My Strength and My Song

365 daily devotional journal

BELLE CITY GIFTS

Belle City Gifts
Savage, Minnesota, USA
Belle City Gifts is an imprint of BroadStreet Publishing Group, LLC.
Broadstreetpublishing.com

My Strength and My Song

9781424571260

Typesetting and design by Garborg Design Works | garborgdesign.com
Editorial services by Michelle Winger | literallyprecise.com

Printed in China.

25 26 27 28 29 30 31 7 6 5 4 3 2 1

There's within my heart a melody
Jesus whispers sweet and low,
Fear not, I am with thee,
peace, be still,
In all of life's ebb and flow.
Jesus, Jesus, Jesus,
Sweetest name I know,
Fills my ev'ry longing,
Keeps me singing as I go.
Feasting on the riches of His grace,
Resting 'neath His shelt'ring wing,
Always looking on His smiling face,
That is why I shout and sing.

He Keeps Me Singing
By L. B. Bridges

Introduction

Deepen your relationship with God and cultivate a more intentional devotional life.

My Strength and My Song is the perfect companion for your daily faith journey. With carefully selected Scriptures, thought-provoking meditations, and guided prompts, this journal will help you center your heart and mind on truth. Slow down, reflect, and align your thoughts with God's Word. As you do, take some time to journal your insights and prayers in the space provided.

Whether you're new to journaling or looking for a fresh approach to your daily devotions, this beautifully designed devotional journal will help you build consistent habits that keep you grounded in your spiritual walk. Lean into the faithfulness of God, experience the joy of his presence, and remember that he is your strength and your song.

DAY 1

All Things New

He who sat on the throne said, "Behold, I make all things new."
And He said to me, "Write, for these words are true and faithful."

REVELATION 21:5 NKJV

The most wonderful thing about the God you've entrusted your life to is that he makes all things new. That is a faithful statement; it has always been and will always be true. Regrets, mistakes, and failures are nothing compared to his covenanted promise of redemption.

What new things are you hoping to do?

DAY 2

New Every Morning

His mercies never end.
They are new every morning.

LAMENTATIONS 3:22-23 CSB

It is beautiful to know that the mercies of God are new every morning. To know that the grace you spent yesterday will still be abundant enough for the troubles you face today. To know that his faithfulness is true even when you wander, and his love is steadfast even when yours fails.

How can you walk as one who knows God's faithfulness and understands his love?

DAY 3

Getting Back

You must return to your God. Maintain love and justice,
and always put your hope in God.

Hosea 12:6 CSB

It's easy to lose your way and lose sight of the passion you once felt for God. Once you've lost your connection with him, you might wonder how to get back. It's as simple as getting down on your knees, opening your heart, and saying, "God, I'm back."

In what ways have you wandered from God?

DAY 4

The Secrets of God

"Can you understand the secrets of God?
Can you search the limits of the Almighty?"

Job 11:7 NCV

Have you ever discovered something about yourself that you never knew before? If you, who are human, are so complex that you don't fully know yourself, then how much more complex is the God who created you? You cannot know his limits, but you can trust in his Word.

How might you be limiting God?

DAY 5

The Yes

The yes to all of God's promises is in Christ,
and through Christ we say yes to the glory of God.

2 Corinthians 1:20 NCV

Everyone goes through seasons in life when they doubt if God is really good. But tasting the goodness of God is often as simple as opening your heart to receive what he has promised. You may feel unworthy, but if you have said yes to salvation, then you have also said yes to his goodness.

What goodness have you received from God recently?

DAY 6

Filling Hunger

"I am the bread of life.... No one who comes to me will ever be hungry,
and no one who believes in me will ever be thirsty again."

John 6:35 CSB

Everyone was created with a spiritual hunger for God. But they must learn how to fill that hunger. There are things that you may put into your soul that will never satisfy you. The only true remedy to the deepest longing in your being is connection with God.

How do you connect with God?

DAY 7

Powerful Words

"Son of man, let all my words sink deep into your own heart first. Listen to them carefully for yourself."

EZEKIEL 3:10 NLT

There is so much power in quieting your mind and listening to the voice of God. He has the power and the ability to speak to any situation you are going through. He has begun powerful works with a simple word. Listen carefully for him.

How do you practice listening to God?

REFLECTIONS OF THE WEEK

DAY 8

Standing at the Last

In perfect faithfulness you have done wonderful things,
things planned long ago.

Isaiah 25:1 NIV

It's easy to become discouraged in this life, but when you adjust your perspective to view everything against the backdrop of a victorious Savior, you can face absolutely anything with great confidence and peace.

How can you walk assured of your victory in Christ?

DAY 9

Water and Blood

This is He who came by water and blood—Jesus Christ;
not only by water, but by water and blood.

1 John 5:6 NKJV

Jesus didn't come to earth only to save; he also came to heal. He takes you as you are, but he doesn't leave you that way. Jesus came with water to cleanse you from sin and heal you from the inside out. He came with blood, trading his life for yours. Your salvation is complete!

How often do you thank God for his salvation and healing?

DAY 10

Out of Darkness

Proclaim the excellencies of Him who has called you
out of darkness into His marvelous light.

1 Peter 2:9 NASB

Don't try to hide where you came from. No matter how dark or shameful your past was before you met Christ, there is power in your testimony. You have been chosen to proclaim God's excellence and to be the visible evidence of his marvelous, life-changing light.

How can you be a light today?

DAY 11

Unpunished

He has not punished us as our sins should be punished;
he has not repaid us for the evil we have done.

Psalm 103:10 NCV

Through the grace of salvation, you have life, reward, and relationship with God. While the devil condemns and causes you to think that you have lost favor with God, the Holy Spirit convicts and leads you to repentance and greater favor.

What is the difference between condemnation and conviction?

DAY 12

Believe It

"Everyone who lives and believes in me shall never die.
Do you believe this?"

JOHN 11:26 ESV

You might be accustomed to promises being made and broken daily. Human fallacy has left some skeptical and anxious. The beautiful truth is that you serve a God who will never back out of his covenant. Your hope of eternal life is sealed when you place your trust in Christ.

Do you believe in the hope of eternal life with Christ?

DAY 13

Accomplishment

LORD, you will grant us peace;
all we have accomplished is really from you.

ISAIAH 26:12 NLT

As you look back on your life, you might remember what you've accomplished with some sense of pride. As you reflect, you must know that you could have done none of it without God. He is the one who carries your burdens, comforts your heart, strengthens your resolve, and orders your steps.

What has God accomplished in your life?

DAY 14

Unseen

We do not focus on what is seen, but on what is unseen.
For what is seen is temporary, but what is unseen is eternal.

2 Corinthians 4:18 CSB

It's not easy to fix your eyes on something you can't see. By abandoning your earthly perspective and exchanging it for a heavenly one, you are radically changed. If you fix your eyes on the promise of heaven, then you cannot help but be filled with peace, joy, and hope.

How can you focus on what is unseen?

REFLECTIONS OF THE WEEK

DAY 15

Faithful

Let us hold fast the confession of our hope without wavering,
for he who promised is faithful.

HEBREWS 10:23 ESV

You don't have to question whether or not God will do what he says. Through the power of the Holy Spirit, the truth of the Word of God, and the encouragement of fellow believers, you can hold fast to the hope of your salvation, staying true to the confession you made when you first believed.

How have you seen God's faithfulness in your life?

DAY 16

Measured Days

"LORD, make me aware of my end and the number of my days
so that I will know how short-lived I am."

PSALM 39:4 CSB

When you are living a rushed, hectic life, you may forget the age-old reality that life passes very quickly. By numbering your days and being mindful of your fleeting existence on earth, you can spend your energies on the purposes of heaven, which will last forever.

How can you measure your days?

DAY 17

Not Shaken

Cast your burden upon the LORD and He will sustain you;
He will never allow the righteous to be shaken.

PSALM 55:22 NASB

Everyone has different ways of dealing with worry. Some internalize it, others call a friend, and still others find a way to take their minds off it. When you bring your worry to God and lay your anxious heart before him, he will encourage you, lift you up, and sustain you.

What burden do you need to cast on God today?

DAY 18

Never Disappointed

This hope will never disappoint us, because God has
poured out his love to fill our hearts.

ROMANS 5:5 NCV

No one is a stranger to being disappointed. In life, you have likely learned to prepare for both the best and the worst possible outcomes. But when it comes to your salvation, there is no need to brace for disappointment; the hope you have in Christ is guaranteed.

What do you do when you feel disappointed?

DAY 19

Remember Wonders

I will remember the deeds of the LORD;
yes, I will remember your wonders of old.

PSALM 77:11 ESV

When you find yourself doubting God's power to work miracles in your life, you must remember the wonders he has performed throughout history. Believe God for something great, knowing that his power has never lessened, and his wonders never cease.

What wonders have you seen God perform?

DAY 20

Because of the Poor

"I will now rise up, because the poor are being hurt....
I will give them the help they want."

PSALM 12:5 NCV

God's economy is opposite of the world's. Human currency is money and power, while God's is mercy and grace. He is a defender of the helpless and a protector of the weak. If you desire to please the heart of the Father, take up the cause of the poor.

How can you help someone in need?

DAY 21

Fully Devoted

"Where you go I will go, and where you stay I will stay.
Your people will be my people and your God my God."

RUTH 1:16 NIV

Ruth gave up everything she'd ever known to follow Naomi back to Bethlehem—a land completely foreign to her. What a radical commitment! God will reward and repay. Everything you give up for his kingdom will be restored to you in an even greater measure.

Are you willing to leave everything to follow God?

REFLECTIONS OF THE WEEK

DAY 22

Human Empathy

Rejoice with those who rejoice,
weep with those who weep.

ROMANS 12:15 ESV

The power of human empathy is remarkable. When someone is hurt, you can feel their pain. When someone laughs, you can enjoy the moment though the happiness is not your own. As you shoulder others' sorrows and sharing in their joy, you express God's heart to the world.

What is your capacity for empathy?

DAY 23

Make a Change

Be transformed by the renewing of your mind. Then you will be able to test and approve what God's will is—his good, pleasing and perfect will.

ROMANS 12:2 NIV

You want change, but you struggle to get (or stay) on task with your goals. While doing great things is appealing, the comfort of doing nothing seems safe. The center of God's will truly is the safest place. Revel in him as he molds and inspires you. You were created to do good things.

What good things would you like to do?

DAY 24

He Cares

In Christ we, though many, form one body,
and each member belongs to all the others.

Romans 12:5 NIV

Everyone is created to carry different aspects of God's glory. Take up your unique gifts and allow others to do the same. When you finally embrace your interdependence, you honor others and contribute to unity. Embrace who you are in Christ and let go of what you are not.

How can you foster your God-given gifts?

DAY 25

Leveling Up

In all your ways acknowledge him,
and he will make straight your paths.

Proverbs 3:6 ESV

As you learn to walk in surrender to the Holy Spirit, your heavenly Father beckons you to a deeper level of intimacy. Be vulnerable with him. When you trust God without boundaries, you find him more reliable than anyone else.

How can you acknowledge God in your life today?

DAY 26

Filled Up

I pray that the God who gives hope will fill you
with much joy and peace while you trust in him.

ROMANS 15:13 NCV

Life's challenges can quickly drain you of your strength. If your hope is in God, you have a source of refreshing. When you turn to the promises found in his Word and the joy found in his presence, you will be revived by his Spirit and filled with peace.

Where do you go to get refreshed?

DAY 27

Freedom

It is for freedom that Christ has set us free. Stand firm, then,
and do not let yourselves be burdened again by a yoke of slavery.

GALATIANS 5:1 NIV

Christ paid a very high price for your freedom. With his life, he purchased your salvation and your emancipation from sin. Stand firm in the truth of your privilege, walking confidently in the freedom that was so dearly bought for you.

How do you stay away from the yoke of sin?

DAY 28

Power to Transform

We are made right with God by placing our faith in Jesus Christ.
And this is true for everyone who believes, no matter who we are.

ROMANS 3:22 NLT

God has the power to transform anything. You may think a person or situation is completely beyond redemption, but God can reclaim even the most impossible of hearts and circumstances. He can certainly intervene in a situation and have his way in it.

Who are you believing for God to transform?

REFLECTIONS OF THE WEEK

DAY 29

Irony of Weakness

He gives power to the weak
and strength to the powerless.

Isaiah 40:29 NLT

When you are stripped of your talents and strengths, you can do nothing but rely on the grace of God to carry you. It is there, in your lack, that God's power is truly revealed. If your inadequacy can further reveal Christ in you, it is always worth it.

Where do you most see God's power in your life?

DAY 30

Weight of Worry

Anxiety in a man's heart weighs him down,
but a good word makes him glad.

Proverbs 12:25 ESV

Worry fills your head with questions that may never have answers and possibilities that may never come to pass. In these times, the encouraging words of a friend can become the catalyst to change your uncertainty into strength and your doubt into restored faith.

Which of your friends speaks truth to your heart?

DAY 31

Joyful Remembrance

The LORD had done great things for us;
we were joyful.

PSALM 126:3 CSB

The tapestry of your life has been beautifully woven with a million moments of grace and wonder. Think back for a moment on some of the things God has done for you. Remembering the miraculous amidst the ordinary strengthens you as you rejoice in the great things he has done.

What great things has God done for you?

DAY 32

Guided

I will lead the blind by a way they did not know;
I will guide them on paths they have not known.

ISAIAH 42:16 CSB

When you think you have lost your way, and you can't feel the path beneath you, God promises that he will lead you forward. Even if you can't see what lies ahead, and though the road feels rocky and unsure, God will guide you.

What path do you need God to guide you on?

DAY 33

Set Apart Truth

"Sanctify them in the truth;
Your word is truth."

JOHN 17:17 NASB

Society is bombarded with falsehood daily. Tabloids tout lies, newspapers print inaccuracies, shows muddy reality, and social media is littered with fake news. In a world of misinformation, there is one source of truth that you can always trust—the Bible.

How do you establish yourself in the truth?

DAY 34

God of Safety

Those who go to God Most High for safety
will be protected by the Almighty.

PSALM 91:1 NCV

Everyone applauds the heroism of David when he took on Goliath and the boldness of Moses when he confronted Pharaoh about freeing the Israelites. Do you know the same safety has been given to you? Whatever you are facing right now, God is more than able to protect you.

When do you turn to God for safety?

DAY 35

Him Alone

You must follow the LORD your God and fear him. You must keep his commands and listen to him; you must worship him and remain faithful to him.

DEUTERONOMY 13:4 CSB

God is gracious and kind, but he is also jealous. Passionate causes, exciting ideas, and energizing visions can sometimes distract you from the one purpose that should hold your allegiance—following God. Let your devotion to him be the defining cause of your life.

How can you prioritize God more?

REFLECTIONS OF THE WEEK

DAY 36

Cleansed

Wash me thoroughly from my iniquity,
And cleanse me from my sin.

PSALM 51:2 NKJV

In the cleansing of your iniquity, you are brought nearer to God. When you compare sin to the treasure of closeness with the Father, it instantly loses its worth. God doesn't harden his heart to a repentant believer. When you cry out to him in genuine remorse, he will restore you.

What sin do you need removed?

DAY 37

Without Fear

She is clothed with strength and dignity,
and she laughs without fear of the future.

PROVERBS 31:25 NLT

It can be frightening when you don't know what's coming or how to prepare for it. But you don't have to fear the future. You can live without anxiety about what is to come because you know that your life is in the hands of the Creator of everything.

What fear can you let go of today?

DAY 38

A Greater Wonder

When I look at your heavens, the work of your fingers…
what is man that you are mindful of him?

Psalm 8:3-4 ESV

The greatness of God is displayed majestically throughout his creation. When you look at all the twinkling stars and the far-off planets, you realize how small you are in his universe. A greater wonder than this is his value for mankind. His love for you is as unsearchable as the heavens.

Are you surprised by God's value of you?

DAY 39

Fully Committed

"May your hearts be fully committed to the Lord your God,
to live by his decrees and obey his commands, as at this time."

1 Kings 8:61 NIV

Is your heart fully committed to God, or are other loves claiming your devotion? If your heart has truly been given to the Lord, then you will naturally follow his commands. To be committed to someone is to be driven by a desire to please them, to give them your best.

How do you give God your best?

DAY 40

Trustworthy

The word of the LORD holds true,
and you can trust everything he does.

PSALM 33:4 NLT

You have likely experienced being jaded by failed dreams, broken relationships, and empty promises. No matter how hurt or worn down you may feel, you can always trust God with your heart. He will never lie to you, manipulate you, or let you down. He is always true to his Word.

How well do you trust God?

DAY 41

Go in Peace

Then He said to the woman,
"Your faith has saved you. Go in peace."

LUKE 7:50 NKJV

Each time after Jesus healed someone, he gave them the same command: "Go in peace." Jesus knew that even after the wonder of the miracle, there would be questions. When you come to Christ, you are brought into a life of wholeness and peace. Walk confidently in it!

How can you walk in peace?

DAY 42

Fascination

Those who love your teachings will find true peace,
and nothing will defeat them.

Psalm 119:165 NCV

The natural result of love is fascination. When you fascinate yourself with the Word of God, his wisdom becomes your confidence and his presence your reward.. You cannot be easily subjected to the lies of the enemy when your heart has been saturated in the truth.

What fascinates you about God?

REFLECTIONS OF THE WEEK

DAY 43

Joyfully I Wait

I wait for the Lord, my whole being waits,
and in his word I put my hope.

Psalm 130:5 NIV

Usually waiting is hard. It can even be unpleasant. But it can also be wonderful, like waiting to deliver great news or waiting for the birth of a child. When the thing you wait for is good, waiting itself is a gift. This is how it is to wait for the Lord. With your hope in him, the outcome is certain.

What lessons have you learned while waiting for something?

DAY 44

Though You Stumble

Though he may stumble, he will not fall,
for the Lord upholds him with his hand.

Psalm 37:23-24 NIV

Recall a near miss or two: the accident that almost happened, the plane you almost missed, the storm that began a few seconds after you made it inside. Did you really "almost" fall, or were you given a glimpse of the Lord at work in your life? Take the opportunity to thank him!

How can you see an "almost disaster" as a glimpse of God's love?

DAY 45

Good and Perfect

Whatever is good and perfect is a gift coming down to us from God your Father, who created all the lights in the heavens.

JAMES 1:17 NLT

Take the next few minutes to pause and consider all the beauty in your life. You may be in a season that makes this easy, or perhaps now is a time that doesn't feel particularly good or perfect. Peonies in June, the wink of a quarter moon, loving and being loved, these are gifts from God.

What gifts of God are you thankful for today?

DAY 46

Tears to Joy

Those who sow in tears
shall reap with shouts of joy!

PSALM 126:5 ESV

In times of sadness, it can seem like the pain will never end. No words of comfort, no matter how true or well-intentioned, can take away the ache. These are the times you need only to crawl into your Father's lap and allow his love and promises to envelop you.

How do you feel about this Scripture right now?

DAY 47

Not of the World

"My prayer is not that you take them out of the world but that you protect them from the evil one. They are not of the world, even as I am not of it."

JOHN 17:15-16 NIV

When something is too wonderful to describe, you might say it is "out of this world." Something sets it apart as special. There is something different about those who belong to Jesus. They are no longer of this world. They are special, and they are protected by God.

How are you different than those in the world?

DAY 48

Under His Protection

He will order his angels
to protect you wherever you go.

PSALM 91:11 NLT

Safety is big business. Consider all the product lines that exist to protect you: everything from sports equipment to security systems. God knows your desire for security, and he offers protection like none other. He's got your eternal soul under his wing.

When have you most sensed God's protection?

DAY 49

People of Light

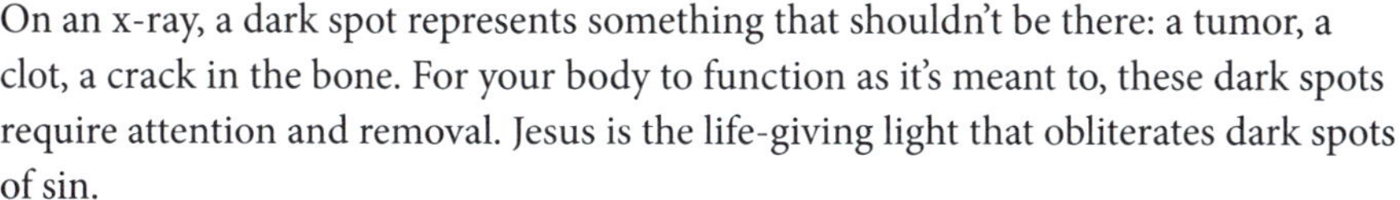

Live as people of light! For this light within you
produces only what is good and right and true.

EPHESIANS 5:8-9 NLT

On an x-ray, a dark spot represents something that shouldn't be there: a tumor, a clot, a crack in the bone. For your body to function as it's meant to, these dark spots require attention and removal. Jesus is the life-giving light that obliterates dark spots of sin.

What dark areas need light in your life?

REFLECTIONS OF THE WEEK

DAY 50

Truly Awesome

The heavens declare the glory of God;
the skies proclaim the work of his hands.

PSALM 19:1 NIV

Amazing beauty is everywhere. When was the last time you stopped to marvel at God's incredible creativity? Study a flower. Read about the human eye. Watch the sun rise or set. Spend some time soaking in the awesomeness of the Creator.

What has inspired awe in you lately?

DAY 51

All of You

"Love the Lord your God with all your heart and with all your soul and with all your mind and with all your strength."

MARK 12:30 NIV

Do you know how desperately the Father loves you? Replacing the myriad rules of the Old Testament, Jesus says to keep one beautiful commandment: love God with your entire being. He wants to be loved with your heart, your soul, your mind, and your strength.

Which of these are you most reluctant to give him?

DAY 52

Rocks Don't Change

Trust in the LORD forever,
for the LORD, the LORD himself, is the Rock eternal.

ISAIAH 26:4 NIV

When people talk about the most dependable person they know, they may describe that person as being a rock. Rocks don't change, and neither do these people. They represent a constant; their principles—and their love—are unwavering.

What does it mean to have God as your rock?

DAY 53

Rest for Your Soul

"Take my yoke upon you and learn from me, for I am gentle and humble in heart,
and you will find rest for your souls."

MATTHEW 11:29 NIV

Choose a job: breaking up and moving rocks to prepare a field, or scattering seeds behind the plow. Back-breaking labor or a semi-leisurely stroll? Jesus' invitation to walk with him is such a choice. When he invites you to follow him, he invites you to lighten your load.

How can you find rest for your soul?

DAY 54

Nothing to Fear

In the multitude of my anxieties within me,
Your comforts delight my soul.

PSALM 94:19 NKJV

Worry. Stress. Anxiety. Chances are, just reading those words heightened your own levels of each. Fear is one of the greatest threats to the peace you have. Don't take your eyes off the comforter of your soul: God's Holy Spirit. Turn to him and watch your worries fade away.

What do you need comfort for right now?

DAY 55

Completely Attuned

When I said, "My foot is slipping,"
your unfailing love, LORD, supported me.

PSALM 94:18 NIV

A good surgical assistant knows what instrument the surgeon needs before they ask for it. A mother can spot a broken heart the minute her child enters the room. Attentiveness is part of the job. God is even more attuned to your needs, and he is always with you.

How have you felt God's attention on you lately?

DAY 56

Peace with God

Since you have been justified through faith, you have peace with God through your Lord Jesus Christ.

Romans 5:1 NIV

Do you ever wonder if you please God? For a child of God, it should be an easy answer. Train your heart and mind, so you don't needlessly torment yourself. Your faith justifies you before God, and this makes him very pleased!

How can you have peace with God?

REFLECTIONS OF THE WEEK

DAY 57

Purpose Fulfilled

The LORD will fulfill his purpose for me;
your steadfast love, O LORD, endures forever.

PSALM 138:8 ESV

God is more intent on fulfilling his purpose for your life than you are. While you might have zeal and passion, you naturally grow weak, lazy, or idle. This can be discouraging, but God is not easily deterred. His love will endure over you forever. He won't give up.

How can you partner with God in fulfilling your purpose?

DAY 58

Life Is a Pilgrimage

Blessed are those whose strength is in you,
whose hearts are set on pilgrimage.

PSALM 84: 5 NIV

Anyone who has walked this Christian journey knows the pilgrimage is not always—or ever—a smoothly paved path. Just because you are headed to Zion does not mean you won't struggle. As you let your strength come from God, you will be able to continue.

What spiritual growth have you experienced lately?

DAY 59

Rooted in Love

You, Lord, are a compassionate and gracious God,
slow to anger and abounding in faithful love.

Psalm 86:15 CSB

If your roots are buried deep in the soil of God's love, and you drink all your sustenance through those roots, you will remain confident of his love. You will receive correction and direction from him without offense because you know it comes from a heart of love.

How can you be confident in the love of God?

DAY 60

Unconditional Acceptance

Accept one another, then, just as Christ accepted you,
in order to bring praise to God.

Romans 15:7 NIV

It's easy to list the ways other people could change for the better. You are called to live in harmony, but sometimes "others" can make it difficult. Jesus takes you as you are: broken, imperfect, and sinful. Can you do the same?

How can you accept others as they are?

DAY 61

Ready to See

Open my eyes that I may see
wonderful things in your law.

PSALM 119:18 NIV

Think back to a time you suddenly understood something—an "aha" moment. The Bible is filled with those. As you go deeper into the Word, God opens your eyes to things you never noticed before. Look for the beauty and depth hidden within his Word.

What new insights have you gleaned from the Bible?

DAY 62

A Heart That Cares

God is working in you, giving you the desire
and the power to do what pleases him.

PHILIPPIANS 2:13 NLT

What was your last random act of kindness? These impulses are evidence of the Spirit at work in your life. The more you tune into God, the more he will work in you. Look to him for inspiration and he will provide opportunities to express his love.

What opportunities do you have to be kind?

DAY 63

Twig by Twig

The wise woman builds her house,
But the foolish pulls it down with her hands.

PROVERBS 14:1 NKJV

If you were to see a mother bird ripping her nest apart, how would you react? Choice by choice, twig by twig, you have the option to build or destroy your home, your life, your relationships. Keep your attention on the Father, and he will give you the strength to keep building.

How can you be a builder today?

REFLECTIONS OF THE WEEK

REFLECTIONS

REFLECTIONS

DAY 64

Just Because

Honor the Lord for the glory of his name.
Worship the Lord in the splendor of his holiness.

Psalm 29:2 NLT

It isn't your birthday, but there's a gift on the counter with your name on it. It feels wonderful. When was the last time you worshipped God just for being God? He loves to receive spontaneous gifts of love and honor just as much as you do.

How can you honor God in this moment?

DAY 65

Sight Unseen

Even though you do not see him now, you believe in him and are filled with an inexpressible and glorious joy.

1 Peter 1:8 NIV

How did you first fall in love with Jesus? Unlike human love, one of the great mysteries of faith is how you can know so surely and love so deeply someone you've never actually seen. But you can, and one of the great rewards of faith is inexpressible and glorious joy.

How is your faith producing joy?

DAY 66

Cookie Jar Prayers

"If my people… will humble themselves and pray and seek my face and turn from their wicked ways, then I will hear from heaven."

2 CHRONICLES 7:14 NIV

Even young children understand cause and effect. *If I am naughty, I get a time out. If I say please, I get a cookie.* Do you approach prayer the same way? Humbly seek God's face and turn from your sins so you can be forgiven and heard.

What are you praying for right now?

DAY 67

He Never Sleeps

He will not let you stumble;
the one who watches over you will not slumber.

PSALM 121:3 NLT

How long can you go without sleep? No matter how important the task, how critical the vigil, you have to take a break eventually. God doesn't. He never stops watching. Always and forever, night and day, he's got you.

How are you comforted by this promise?

DAY 68

No Darkness

This is the message you have heard from him and declare to you:
God is light; in him there is no darkness at all.

1 JOHN 1:5 NIV

In total darkness, you instinctively seek light: turn on your phone, fumble for a light switch, light a candle. With a single light source, the darkness can be overcome. You can find your way. God is pure light, and with him, you can overcome any darkness you face.

What situation do you need light for today?

DAY 69

He Chose You

The LORD is all I need.
He takes care of me.

PSALM 16:5 NCV

God chose precisely when and how to invite you to join his family. You received the most prestigious, coveted invitation in history. He chose you. Regardless of how it happened, he called you by name, and now you are his.

When did you accept God's invitation?

DAY 70

Hidden Treasure

He opened their minds so they could
understand the Scriptures.

LUKE 24:45 NIV

It's amazing to watch a movie or read a book you remember from childhood and see all you missed back then. Your mind understands layers of context that you couldn't as a child. In a similar way, the Bible can feel brand new every time you read it.

How do you discover treasures in God's Word?

REFLECTIONS OF THE WEEK

DAY 71

More of You

"He must become greater;
I must become less."

JOHN 3:30 NIV

Imagine you're famous. People follow you, listen to you, and genuinely respect you. Now, imagine willingly, even happily, giving it all up. Humility is hard. It's also a requirement for a Christ-centered life.

How can you become less?

DAY 72

An Incomprehensible Gift

People are counted as righteous, not because of their work,
but because of their faith in God who forgives sinners.

ROMANS 4:4-5 NLT

In an employment agreement, both parties have to honor their part for it to work. This is what makes your relationship—your agreement—with Jesus so astonishing. His part was death on a cross to ensure your salvation. Your part is believing that is true.

How often do you thank God for your salvation?

DAY 73

Where You Are

Then the LORD God called to the man,
"Where are you?"

GENESIS 3:9 NLT

When adults play hide-and-seek with children, they usually know where the kids are hiding. Still, they play along. God knew exactly where Adam and Eve were, but for the healing process to begin, they had to confess. He asked for their benefit.

Where are you?

DAY 74

He Holds My Hand

"I, the LORD your God,
hold your right hand."

ISAIAH 41:13 ESV

Looking back on the hardest, scariest things you've done, you may wonder where you found the courage. Scripture assures you that your help comes from God That sudden burst of strength, bravery, or initiative? That was him, squeezing your hand.

When did God help you be brave?

DAY 75

Not for Nothing

I do not set aside the grace of God, for if righteousness could be gained through the law, Christ died for nothing!

Galatians 2:21 NIV

For weeks you've prepared: study sessions, flash cards, copious notes. You enter the classroom and find out the test is canceled. All that work for nothing. If you believe you can get to heaven by working hard, Jesus' brutal death was pointless. Accept his gift of grace today!

How do you acknowledge Christ's sacrifice?

DAY 76

You Are Chosen

God decided in advance to adopt us into his own family… through Jesus Christ. This is what he wanted to do, and it gave him great pleasure.

Ephesians 1:5 NLT

As a child of God, you are granted the wonderful knowledge of being chosen. You didn't have to accomplish any great feat or fulfill a grand purpose. He just wanted you for himself. You are a great delight to him.

How can you delight in being chosen?

DAY 77

Sheltered

He will shelter you with his wings.
His faithful promises are your armor and protection.

PSALM 91:4 NLT

Like an eagle, God shelters you from storms and attacks. The image is powerful yet tender. How wonderful it is to be tucked right up against him, absorbing his warmth! Don't leave the nest in an attempt to take care of yourself. Accept his protection!

How can you rest in God's promise of protection?

REFLECTIONS OF THE WEEK

DAY 78

Carry Your Shield

In all circumstances take up the shield of faith, with which you can extinguish all the flaming darts of the evil one.

EPHESIANS 6:16 ESV

The shield of faith allows you to quench flaming arrows, but only if you hold it up. It's your responsibility to hold onto your faith and carry it wherever you go. Setting it down, even briefly, leaves you vulnerable to attack.

How do you carry your shield of faith?

DAY 79

Just Say No

Submit yourselves, then, to God.
Resist the devil, and he will flee from you.

JAMES 4:7 NIV

Submit to God; resist the devil. It seems simple. How often do you give in to temptation and resist the one leading you to your best life? Surrender your life to the one who wants only good, peace, and light for you.

How do you choose light over darkness?

DAY 80

Live at Peace

If it is possible, as far as it depends on you,
live at peace with everyone.

Romans 12:18 NIV

Some people get along with almost everyone, for others it's more difficult. Live at peace with everyone? That seems like a pretty big ask. You can't control other people, but with Christ's help, you can control your response. Choose peace today!

How easy is it for you to choose peace?

DAY 81

Peace and Quiet

The work of righteousness will be peace,
And the effect of righteousness, quietness and assurance forever.

Isaiah 32:17 NKJV

Peace and *quiet*. Just saying those words together can bring comfort. Through righteousness comes peace, quietness, and assurance. *Forever.* Righteousness is not an unattainable ideal of perfection or superiority. It's about putting God first, and living in a way that honors him.

How do you strive for righteousness?

DAY 82

Desire to Know

As you do not know the path of the wind…
so you cannot understand the work of God.

ECCLESIASTES 11:5 NIV

"Why?" A toddler who has just grasped the power of this word will say it over and over again. You may have stopped asking it out loud, but you maintain a powerful desire to know. Embrace the reality that you can't know the mind of God, but you can trust him!

How can you rest in not knowing why?

DAY 83

Coffee with God

I rise before dawn and cry for help;
I wait for Your words.

PSALM 119:147 NASB

Do you rise before you need to, eager to start your day, or is the snooze button your best friend? Do you begin your day with God either way? Rewiring may be in order if you can't find time to spend with God. Make it a coffee date with him each day!

How can you prioritize time with God?

DAY 84

Spirited Worship

"God is Spirit, so those who worship him
must worship in spirit and in truth."

JOHN 4:24 NLT

A feisty horse is considered spirited. An athlete overcoming hardship is said to have an indomitable spirit. A spirit goes beyond the physical. God's Holy Spirit is your intimate companion, teacher, and comforter, and he is wholly deserving of your worship.

How do you connect with the Holy Spirit?

REFLECTIONS OF THE WEEK

DAY 85

Real Love

No eye has seen any God besides you,
who acts on behalf of those who wait for him.

Isaiah 64:4 NIV

Authenticity. It matters. Is the gem, the handbag, the promise real? You scrutinize the people and possessions in your lives, looking for authenticity. What great comfort you can take in the one, true God! His love is unfailing, and all his gifts are good.

What does authenticity mean to you?

DAY 86

Foolish Ones

"The eyes of the Lord search the whole earth in order to strengthen those whose hearts are fully committed to him."

2 Chronicles 16:9 NLT

You blew it. Those three words carry a weight no one wishes to bear. That actions have consequences is a hard, painful truth. Perhaps you are living it now. Be encouraged. You will face many trials, but you need never face them alone. Let God be your strength.

How can you show commitment today?

DAY 87

Tell Your Story

Let the redeemed of the Lord tell their story—
those he redeemed from the hand of the foe.

Psalm 107:2 NIV

Whether your story is so complex you barely know where to begin, or you think it's too insignificant to tell, it matters. From the beginning, God had you in mind. He planned the tiniest detail with extravagant love. Begin telling yourself this and be ready to share it with others.

What's your story?

DAY 88

Self-Importance

Humble yourselves under the mighty power of God,
and at the right time he will lift you up in honor.

1 Peter 5:6 NLT

Traffic jams. Grocery store lines. The DMV. Unless you were born with the "patience of a saint," waiting is, at best, an inconvenience. Pondering patience leads to another uncomfortable concept: humility. Is your time really more valuable than everyone else's?

Do you think you are more important than others?

DAY 89

Written in Stone

God's truth stands firm like a foundation stone with this inscription:
"The LORD knows those who are his."

2 TIMOTHY 2:19 NLT

In his second letter to Timothy, Paul shares an important truth in two parts. First, the Lord knows you as his own. Second, those who are his must turn from sin. This matters enough to be written in stone.

What things do you think are written in stone?

DAY 90

Surrender

"Be strong! Let's prove ourselves strong for your people
and for the cities of your God."

1 CHRONICLES 19:13 CSB

Is surrender to God's plan easy for you or a constant challenge? In the words of Joab, you'll find a perfect example of the surrendered life: be strong for those you serve, be courageous for the Kingdom of God, and may the Lord's will be done.

How do you feel about Joab's words?

DAY 91

Fool for You

The message of the cross is foolishness to those who are perishing, but to us who are being saved it is the power of God.

1 Corinthians 1:18 NIV

You've probably had times where your faith has been ridiculed. In these times, it is good to be reminded that human wisdom is nothing compared to God's wisdom. True wisdom seems like foolishness to the world, but to you it is access to the power of God.

How can you be a fool for Jesus?

REFLECTIONS OF THE WEEK

DAY 92

I Am Found

"Rejoice with me;
I have found my lost sheep."

LUKE 15:6 NIV

How pleasing it is to find something you thought you had lost. You rejoice in the small victories of finding a lost receipt, a pair of sunglasses, or that matching sock! Something in your nature tells you loss is to be grieved, and discovery is to be celebrated. You are found in Jesus!

How do you celebrate being found?

DAY 93

Blotted Out

"I, even I, am He who blots out your transgressions for My own sake;
And I will not remember your sins."

ISAIAH 43:25 NKJV

God was merciful to his beloved people who turned away from him many times. His love was enough to forget their sins. He didn't just cover them up, he completely removed them. How incredible to know that God removes your sins.

How will you thank God for covering your sin?

DAY 94

Citizens of Heaven

Our citizenship is in heaven, from which you also eagerly wait for the Savior, the Lord Jesus Christ.

PHILIPPIANS 3:20 NKJV

How great it is to be reminded of home when you are far from it. Sometimes a familiar voice, smell, or picture is enough to trigger a longing to return to where you belong. Eternity is in your heart because you were made for the same glory as Jesus! Heaven is your home.

What are you hoping to experience in heaven?

DAY 95

Heart of Compassion

Jesus, when He came out, saw a great multitude and was moved with compassion for them, because they were like sheep not having a shepherd.

MARK 6:34 NKJV

When Jesus saw the crowds, he didn't just see them as a bothersome multitude, he saw them as people with needs. Like sheep without a shepherd, people are lost, and they need your help. Because you know Jesus, you can have compassion on them.

Who can you help today?

DAY 96

Sing

Sing praises to God, sing praises!
Sing praises to your King, sing praises!

PSALM 47:6 NKJV

You may not have the voice of an angel, but you can sing. God created you with a voice and with lips that can praise him for all the good things he has done. He will delight in your song of praise even if he is the only one who appreciates it!

When do you sing for God?

DAY 97

Powerful Promises

He did not waver through unbelief regarding the promise of God…
fully persuaded that God had power to do what he had promised.

ROMANS 4:20-21 NIV

You serve a God who is more than able to carry out his promises! When you have a revelation of the power of God, your faith will be strengthened and you will have confidence in God's promises to you, and to this world.

What promises are you waiting to see fulfilled?

DAY 98

Everlasting Beauty

Charm is deceitful and beauty is passing,
But a woman who fears the Lord, she shall be praised.

PROVERBS 31:30 NKJV

At some point, you are either going to struggle with jealousy of those who are better looking or with the fact that your outward beauty is fading. The Bible honors those with a heart for God. You will be praised for a heart that moves toward God.

What kind of beauty are you chasing?

REFLECTIONS OF THE WEEK

DAY 99

Opened and Lifted

The LORD opens the eyes of the blind;
The LORD raises up those who are bowed down.

PSALM 146:8 NASB

When Jesus came to earth, he healed many physical and spiritual needs. He opened eyes to the truth, ministered to the poor in spirit, and restored believers to righteousness. God will always lift you up in times of trouble. Let him be your strength today.

How has God opened your eyes?

DAY 100

Be Teachable

Instruct the wise and they will be wiser still;
teach the righteous and they will add to their learning.

PROVERBS 9:9 NIV

A wise person is not just one who has a lot of knowledge. The wise listen to instruction; they continue to seek out wise ways. They want to add to the truth they already know. God delights in your pursuit of him, and he will instruct and teach you to be wiser still!

How do you open your heart to receive instruction?

DAY 101

Peace Seeds

The seed whose fruit is righteousness is sown in peace
by those who make peace.

JAMES 3:18 NASB

There are times when conflict cannot be avoided, but assuming the role of the peacemaker is far better than getting your own way. To be a peacemaker requires humility and a desire for the greater good. Peaceful ways give birth to righteousness.

How can you bring peace wherever you go?

DAY 102

Very Good

God saw everything that He had made,
and indeed it was very good.

GENESIS 1:31 NKJV

How reassuring it is to know that God's creation was intentionally good. He did not create mistakes or flaws; he created you according to his perfect plan. The next time you find yourself despairing about all the things that have gone wrong, go back to the beginning.

What can you see around you that is good?

DAY 103

No More Pain

He will wipe away every tear from their eyes, and death shall be no more, neither shall there be mourning, nor crying, nor pain anymore.

REVELATION 21:4 ESV

There will come a time when there will be no more pain. Life is full of hardship, but you can live in hope that a day will come where joy will reign supreme! Trust that God is still good and that he has good plans for you. Rejoice in eternal life, for this life is not where it ends!

How is your hope restored by this promise?

DAY 104

Brave Heart

"Be strong and courageous! Do not tremble or be dismayed, for the LORD your God is with you wherever you go."

JOSHUA 1:9 NASB

Joshua had a big task to do: lead the entire nation of Israel into the Promised Land. This required defeating great opposition. But when God calls his people to do his will, he empowers them with the ability to do it. He did it for Joshua, and he will do it for you!

What do you need to be brave about now?

DAY 105

Mere Mortals

In God I trust and am not afraid.
What can mere mortals do to me?

PSALM 56:4 NIV

You may not always be spared hurt or pain, but God is always present and promises to take care of you. It is important to remember that no matter what you face, no "mere mortal" can ever take away your eternal destiny in Jesus.

Where is your trust placed?

REFLECTIONS OF THE WEEK

DAY 106

Practice Produces Peace

Do what you have learned and received and heard from me,
and seen in me, and the God of peace will be with you.

PHILIPPIANS 4:9 CSB

Paul was chosen by God to carry the good news of Jesus Christ to all who were willing to receive it. You are blessed to have all of this truth available through the Bible. Keep practicing the things that you have learned through God's Word, and peace will be yours.

What have you been practicing?

DAY 107

Church Siblings

He has given us this command: Anyone who loves God
must also love their brother and sister.

1 JOHN 4:21 NIV

Family members can be some of the hardest people to get along with. And people in your church may not always be easy to love. But when you love God, you obey his commands, and he desires that you have right relationships with his children—your church siblings!

Who can you show love to today?

DAY 108

Starry Host

You alone are the LORD. You made the heavens, even the highest heavens, and all their starry host, the earth and all that is on it, the seas and all that is in them.

NEHEMIAH 9:6 NIV

God made the earth and everything in it, from blades of grass to fiery volcanoes. He created the heavens, the universe, and everything beyond it. There are things you will not get to see or understand while you are limited by your earthly body. God is amazing!

What are you excited to discover in creation?

DAY 109

On Your Behalf

He is able to save completely those who come to God through him, because he always lives to intercede for them.

HEBREWS 7:25 NIV

When Jesus died on the cross and rose again, he not only took the penalty for your sin, he also became the way in which you can approach God boldly. He made you holy, and he intercedes on your behalf to declare you righteous before God.

How can Jesus intercede for you today?

DAY 110

Debt of Love

Let no debt remain outstanding, except the continuing debt to love one another, for whoever loves others has fulfilled the law.

ROMANS 13:8 NIV

When a bill arrives in the mail, you are reminded that you owe money for a product or service. If you leave it for too long, it can cause anxiety and resentment. But some debt is good. The Bible says to treat love as a debt, so you are continually compelled to love.

Who can you love better today?

DAY 111

His Riches

This same God who takes care of me will supply all your needs from his glorious riches, which have been given to us in Christ Jesus.

PHILIPPIANS 4:19 NLT

Riches are found in God's goodness, grace, and sovereignty. He is always able to provide for all your needs. Sometimes you may feel unworthy to receive from him. You are a child of the King, and he offers his riches to you. Trust in his goodness.

What do you need from God right now?

DAY 112

Water Ways

Let justice flow like a river,
and let goodness flow like a never-ending stream.

Amos 5:24 NCV

Referees at sports matches, lines at the store, and a judge in the courtroom all exist to encourage fairness. When you see or experience injustice, you long for it to be made right. God is just. What a blessing it is when his people do what is right.

How can you encourage fairness?

REFLECTIONS OF THE WEEK

DAY 113

Continue in Christ

Just as you received Christ Jesus as Lord,
continue to live your lives in him.

Colossians 2:6 NIV

Receiving Christ causes a wonderful transformation. But there is fullness to the Christian life that goes beyond salvation. The Scripture says that you continue your life in him. This means that every day you have the opportunity to grow in your relationship with God.

How can you grow today?

DAY 114

Lean on the Lord

Trust in the Lord with all your heart,
And lean not on your own understanding.

Proverbs 3:5 NKJV

When you are faced with challenging situations, particularly when you are making big decisions, do you try to figure things out on your own? When that doesn't work, do you pray? Wouldn't it be better if you left it up to God in the first place?

Do you trust the Lord?

DAY 115

Walking in Works

We are His workmanship, created in Christ Jesus for good works, which God prepared beforehand so that we would walk in them.

EPHESIANS 2:10 NASB

God has always had a plan for your life. He created, designed, and brought you into being. He has gifted you with talents, nurtured you, and developed character in you. You are his wonderful workmanship!

What good works were you created for?

DAY 116

Satisfied

I will be fully satisfied as with the richest of foods; with singing lips my mouth will praise you.

PSALM 63:5 NIV

There are times when you really need answers, and sometimes you just want to be blessed. The Father says to simply ask. He wants to give you good gifts. He can handle your requests. His love is better than life itself, and he knows exactly how to satisfy you.

What are you asking God for today?

DAY 117

Holy Spirit Words

"Don't worry about how to defend yourself or what to say. At that time the Holy Spirit will teach you what you must say."

LUKE 12:11-12 NCV

Defending your faith may be a challenge. You might not be dragged into a court over your beliefs, but you can expect to have opposition and confrontation. The Holy Spirit was given as a helper. You can be confident that he will give you the right words when you need them.

When do you most need the right words?

DAY 118

East to West

If I rise with the sun in the east and settle in the west beyond the sea, even there you would guide me.

PSALM 139:9-10 NCV

Moving into a new circumstance, house, or country means you have to leave what is comfortable and step into the unknown. No matter where you go, God will always go with you. He is as far east as the rising sun, and as far west as the sunset.

What new thing are you moving into?

DAY 119

Assignment

My life is worth nothing to me unless I use it for finishing the work assigned me by the Lord Jesus.

ACTS 20:24 NLT

When it is all said and done, there is nothing more important in your life than the good news of Jesus. He came to earth to reveal God's nature. He sacrificed his life to save you. He defeated death. He gives you grace so you can walk in freedom. You have a lot of good news to share!

What is your assignment?

REFLECTIONS OF THE WEEK

DAY 120

Whole Restoration

My whole being, praise the LORD
and do not forget all his kindnesses.

PSALM 103:2 NCV

God is in the business of restoration. He shows kindness by caring for your entire being. Not only does he want to restore a right relationship with you, he also wants to restore your body to health. When you are spiritually or physically weak, don't forget the promises of God.

How can you praise God with your whole being?

DAY 121

Equipped for Battle

Put on the full armor of God, so that you can
take your stand against the devil's schemes.

EPHESIANS 6:11 NIV

At times it is hard to acknowledge that you are in a spiritual battle and that there is opposition to the good works of God. The devil does have his schemes, but God has provided you with everything you need to equip yourself against these schemes.

How do you equip yourself for battle?

DAY 122

Prayer Counts

Pray in the Spirit on all occasions
with all kinds of prayers and requests.

EPHESIANS 6:18 NIV

Maybe you are too analytical with your prayers. You think you ought to make them sound fancy or humble. You might not trust your intentions when you pray, but God sees your heart. He wants you to talk with him in all occasions and with all kinds of prayers.

How will you pray today?

DAY 123

Chased by Grace

Surely goodness and mercy shall follow me
All the days of my life.

PSALM 23:6 NKJV

You leave footprints as you walk the path of life. Some are left from walking in the dirt, and they need to be cleaned up. God wants to lead you in the right direction. As you live in his ways, your path will be followed by goodness, and his mercy will clean up those dirty prints.

What path are you following?

DAY 124

Spiritual Guidance

If we live by the Spirit,
let us also keep in step with the Spirit.

GALATIANS 5:25 CSB

Living by the Spirit means you are continually dying to the sinful desires of your fallen nature. When you surrender your sinful nature to the cross, you produce fruit that is proof of the Spirit working within you.

How do you keep in step with the Spirit?

DAY 125

Key to Success

Then you will live a long time,
and your life will be successful.

PROVERBS 3:2 NCV

Today success is associated with riches and social status. Often, successful people have had access to good teachers and successful strategies for learning well. You can pursue Godly success through Godly wisdom and teaching. You have all you need to live a full life in God!

How do you measure success?

DAY 126

A Patient Promise

The Lord is not slow about His promise… but is patient toward you,
not wishing for any to perish but for all to come to repentance.

2 Peter 3:9 NASB

Jesus will return one day; he promised he would! His return can seem slow to those who are waiting, but if you understand the love that Jesus has for humanity, you can understand his reason for waiting. Be patient in his promise. He will return!

What does patiently waiting look like for you?

REFLECTIONS OF THE WEEK

REFLECTIONS

REFLECTIONS

DAY 127

Pentecost Power

"You shall receive power when the Holy Spirit has come upon you."

ACTS 1:8 NKJV

The Holy Spirit can be a powerful influence in your life. When you genuinely display the power of the Holy Spirit, people will be drawn to your witness of the gospel of Jesus Christ. The same Spirit who came upon the believers on Pentecost is with you today.

Have you experienced the Holy Spirit's power?

DAY 128

Humble Highs

Humble yourselves before the Lord, and he will lift you up.

JAMES 4:10 NIV

It seems an upside-down thing to say; in humility you will be lifted up. Often humility carries a sense of shame. There is no shame, however, in humility before God. The Lord loves humility because it draws you close to him and allows him to work through you.

How can you show humility?

DAY 129

Free of the Past

If anyone is in Christ, he is a new creation; old things have passed away; behold, all things have become new.

2 CORINTHIANS 5:17 NKJV

Before Christ, you were slaves to your sinful nature and had no freedom from the things you had done wrong. When Jesus died on the cross, he took your sin upon himself, and he displayed his victory over it when he rose again. Live as the new creation you are!

What newness do you notice in yourself?

DAY 130

Strength of My Heart

God is the strength of my heart
and my portion forever.

PSALM 73:25-26 NIV

When you begin to understand both the love and the greatness of God, you become convinced that he is everything. He is your all; there is nothing in heaven or earth that is greater. His love for you will give you everything you need. He is your portion forever.

What does "more than enough" look like to you?

DAY 131

Convinced of Love

I am persuaded that neither death nor life… nor any other created thing will be able to separate us from the love of God that is in Christ Jesus our Lord.

ROMANS 8:38-39 CSB

Your relationship with Jesus Christ is eternal. You may have just begun this journey with him, or have been a friend of God your whole life. Whatever your life story, you are covered by his grace and can never be separated from his love.

Are you convinced of God's love?

DAY 132

Opportunity for Joy

When troubles of any kind come your way, consider it an opportunity for great joy.

JAMES 1:2 NLT

It's not easy to approach troubles with joy, unless you understand how things will work out for good. One of the best things that comes from trouble is that you are tested. And while testing seems difficult, when you pass, you have greater confidence.

What opportunities for joy do you have right now?

DAY 133

Quenched

The desert and the parched land will be glad;
the wilderness will rejoice and blossom.

Isaiah 35:1 NIV

There are times in life when you feel like you are always striving and never getting anywhere, where you thirst for something more. God has promised a day when you will no longer thirst for fulfillment. Everything you desire will be satisfied. Look for his oasis in the meantime.

What are you thirsting for?

REFLECTIONS OF THE WEEK

DAY 134

Provision

May He who supplies seed to the sower, and bread for food, supply and multiply the seed you have sown and increase the fruits of your righteousness.

2 CORINTHIANS 9:10 NKJV

Just as a farmer requires seed for a harvest, you must have something to sow in order to reap. God has supplied you with everything you need to help in growing his kingdom. He will increase your resources as you diligently plant the seeds of faith.

What seeds of faith are you planting?

DAY 135

Light of the Dawn

Even in darkness light dawns for the upright,
for those who are gracious and compassionate and righteous.

PSALM 112:4 NIV

In the middle of the night, anxiety can be heightened. Irrational fears, disturbing thoughts, or a disquieted spirit may persist. But the first rays of light often bring peace, hope, and joy. Even in your moments of darkness, God's light will dawn for you.

Where do you most need the light of dawn?

DAY 136

Heavenly Scent

Thanks be to God who always leads us in triumph in Christ, and through us diffuses the fragrance of His knowledge in every place.

2 Corinthians 2:14 NKJV

Jesus Christ has triumphed over sin and death, and you are called to be a part of this victory! He has led you in the battle, and you are on the winning side! The victory of Jesus can be like perfume that diffuses into every place you go. Wear it today!

How do you diffuse the fragrance of Christ?

DAY 137

Thunder Theology

"God's voice thunders in marvelous ways;
he does great things beyond your understanding."

Job 37:5 NIV

Thunder is powerful, mysterious, and commanding. It's little wonder that God's voice is described this way. With it, he created the heavens and the earth, and he can command all things into submission. God is present and powerful. Trust him to do great things.

What great things have you been asking for?

DAY 138

Believing Not Seeing

These things I have written to you who believe in the name of the Son of God, that you may know that you have eternal life, and that you may continue to believe.

1 JOHN 5:13 NKJV

Jesus calls blessed those who have not seen him and yet believe. You are blessed because you love him and have faith in him. This is why you can have joy in the midst of all situations. You have faith in the truth, and it will one day bring you to glory.

How can you believe without seeing?

DAY 139

Fixed on Him

Looking to Jesus, the founder and perfecter of your faith, who for the joy that was set before him endured the cross.

HEBREWS 12:2 ESV

Jesus endured overwhelming suffering by looking toward the joy set before him. He saw beyond his suffering for the purpose of your redemption, and he knew that God would be glorified. When you are going through difficulties, stay focused on Jesus.

How do you keep your focus on Jesus?

DAY 140

Eternal Kingdom

Since you are receiving a Kingdom that is unshakable, let us be thankful and please God by worshiping him with holy fear and awe.

HEBREWS 12:28 NLT

Kings and queens hold their throne for a time, but ultimately their reign ends. The kingdom of God is not like the kingdom of men. It is undefeatable and unshakeable. You belong to God's kingdom, and it will never be defeated.

How often do you thank God for being part of his kingdom?

REFLECTIONS OF THE WEEK

DAY 141

Fiery Furnace

"If you are thrown into the blazing furnace, the God whom you serve is able to save us. He will rescue us from your power, Your Majesty."

DANIEL 3:17 NLT

What confidence Shadrach, Meshach, and Abednego had in God's power to rescue them from the blazing furnace! You are unlikely to have to go through literal flames for God, but he will honor your decision to stand up for your faith in him.

How can you stand up for God?

DAY 142

Evergreen

It doesn't fear when heat comes,
and its foliage remains green.

JEREMIAH 17:8 CSB

Trees that are planted closest to the source of life are strong, healthy, and fruitful. A tree that is not planted near water will struggle to survive when the heat comes. God is your source of life. Draw close to him and let him refresh and sustain you.

Where do you draw strength from?

DAY 143

My Redeemer Lives

"I know that my Redeemer lives,
and at the last he will stand upon the earth."

JOB 19:25 ESV

In the middle of suffering, the only thing that you may be able to hold onto is a declaration. While Job could not comprehend his suffering or God's ways, he knew in his heart and declared with his lips, "My Redeemer lives." Be uplifted as you dwell on that declaration.

What declaration helps you through hardship?

DAY 144

Always Helping

God is not unjust; he will not forget your work and the love you have shown him as you have helped his people and continue to help them.

HEBREWS 6:10 NIV

Do you sometimes feel as though you give and give and are never appreciated? While people may not take the time to appreciate your help, God most certainly will! He does not forget that you have shown love to his people, and he knows that this equates to your love for him.

How is this word encouraging to you?

DAY 145

He Rejoices over You

He will quiet you with His love,
He will rejoice over you with singing.

ZEPHANIAH 3:17 NKJV

It doesn't seem to matter what particular gift a child might have, a parent will always find something in that child to praise. A parent's love is not about what the child can do, but about who they are. Your heavenly Father feels like this about you—only much more!

Who do you rejoice over?

DAY 146

Many Wonders

Many, O LORD my God,
are the wonders you have done.

PSALM 40:5 NIV

It is good to give God glory for all the things that are too wonderful for words. God has acted powerfully on many occasions to preserve his chosen people. You can probably think of many examples of how God has done great things for you. There are likely too many to declare!

What are some of the great things God has done for you?

DAY 147

Thirsty for Mercy

Come, all you who are thirsty,
come to the waters.

ISAIAH 55:1 NIV

Imagine walking into a grocery store and being offered anything you want without having to pay a cent! This is a picture of the mercy that Jesus has shown through his sacrifice. You need God's mercy in the same way you thirst for water, and he has it in abundance.

Are you thirsty for mercy?

REFLECTIONS OF THE WEEK

DAY 148

Divine Decisions

Oh, how great are God's riches and wisdom and knowledge!
How impossible it is for us to understand his decisions and his ways!

ROMANS 11:33 NLT

When you are faced with a significant choice, you can use a variety of strategies to come up with an answer. Some are good and others are not! Let God into your decision-making process and trust his ways. He has wisdom and knowledge beyond your understanding.

What decisions are you making now?

DAY 149

Contentment Always

I know what it is to be in need, and I know what it is to have plenty.
I have learned the secret of being content in any and every situation.

PHILIPPIANS 4:12 NIV

The shortcoming of both poverty and riches is that you always want more. The secret to Paul's contentment was that he had experienced God's provision for his spiritual, emotional, and physical needs and knew he didn't need anything more. You can experience this too!

How do you practice being content?

DAY 150

Radiant Reflection

He is the radiance of the glory of God and the exact imprint of his nature,
and he upholds the universe by the word of his power.

HEBREWS 1:3 ESV

Jesus was no ordinary man. When he came to earth, he revealed God's nature. Because he is the radiance of God, he reflects both power and love. Now seated with God in heaven, he upholds the universe, and he upholds you with his Word.

How are you a reflection of Christ?

DAY 151

Search Me

Search me, O God, and know my heart;
Try me and know my anxious thoughts.

PSALM 139:23 NASB

Searching requires looking in every possible place. Asking God to search your heart means that you are inviting him to know everything in it. Vulnerability is hard, but when you invite him in, you acknowledge that you need his love and guidance.

When did you last ask God to search your heart?

DAY 152

Filled with Delight

Then I was constantly at his side.
I was filled with delight day after day.

Proverbs 8:30 NIV

What does it mean to take delight in being with God? The natural outcome of being in his presence is joy, strength, delight, and a desire to remain there. The more you soak in his Word and cultivate your relationship with him, the more he will delight and satisfy you.

When do you spend time at God's side?

DAY 153

Inner Beauty

Your beauty should come from within you—the beauty of a gentle and quiet spirit that will never be destroyed and is very precious to God.

1 Peter 3:4 NCV

God is enraptured by your inner beauty. What you look like in the mirror will never matter as much as what you look like in your soul. Your human form is not what he fell in love with. The beauty of your spirit is what is precious to him.

How often do you check your inner beauty?

DAY 154

Returned Love

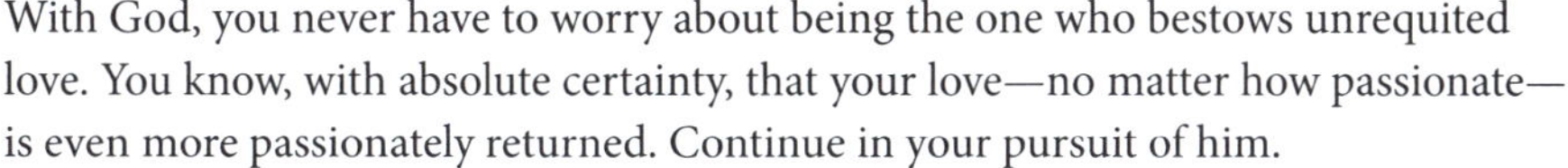

I love those who love me,
and those who seek me find me.

PROVERBS 8:17 NIV

With God, you never have to worry about being the one who bestows unrequited love. You know, with absolute certainty, that your love—no matter how passionate—is even more passionately returned. Continue in your pursuit of him.

How often do you pursue God?

REFLECTIONS OF THE WEEK

DAY 155

Continual Praise

From the rising of the sun to its going down
The LORD's name is to be praised.

PSALM 113:3 NKJV

What would it look like to praise God from the time you woke up until the time you went to sleep? You would effect an incredible change in your personal outlook. Intentional, continual praise naturally results in intentional, continual joy.

What can you praise God for right now?

DAY 156

Powerful Friendship

Flee the evil desires of youth and pursue righteousness, faith, love and peace, along with those who call on the Lord out of a pure heart.

2 TIMOTHY 2:22 NIV

Christians are consistently called to step out of the mold and live differently. Being different isn't easy, but having people around you who are living by the same revolutionary standard ignites passion. Such is the power of friendship!

Who helps keep you passionate about God?

DAY 157

Overcome

"I have told you these things, so that in me you may have peace. In this world you will have trouble. But take heart! I have overcome the world."

JOHN 16:33 NIV

It's easy to feel overwhelmed by all the evil in the world. But when you recognize that God has already conquered it, you can have peace beyond anything imaginable. You can live your life with the strength and confidence that marks a true conqueror.

How will you overcome today?

DAY 158

The Good Father

"And I will be a father to you,
and you shall be sons and daughters to me."

2 CORINTHIANS 6:18 ESV

It's easy to confuse God's majesty with distance. You might begin to think of him as someone who is out of touch, absent, and uninterested. But the opposite is true! God is loving and kind. He takes interest in your deepest thoughts as only a truly good father can.

When do you share your thoughts with God?

DAY 159

Right Relationships

Above all, love each other deeply,
because love covers over a multitude of sins.

1 PETER 4:8 NIV

Love is always the key ingredient for a good relationship because it is synonymous with God. It was the spilled blood of love that blotted out the sins of man, and only that same love can allow two broken people to support one another in godly relationship.

How can you love well?

DAY 160

Joy That Testifies

It was said among the nations,
"The LORD has done great things for them."

PSALM 126:2 NIV

True, joyful worship testifies loudly of God's work in your life. When you praise God for all he has done in your life, the rest of the world will take notice. Take time to praise and thank God joyfully, and the world will not be able to deny the evidence of God's great work.

What testimony can you share today?

DAY 161

Relationships of Believers

Rejoice! Strive for full restoration, encourage one another, be of one mind, live in peace. And the God of love and peace will be with you.

2 CORINTHIANS 13:11 NIV

Engaging in healthy, godly relationships is not easy, especially when there is conflict. It can be almost automatic for us to run the other way. When you strive for unity and restoration, offering encouragement and peace, you welcome the presence of God into your relationships.

What is your relationship with other believers like?

REFLECTIONS OF THE WEEK

DAY 162

Gracious

The LORD longs to be gracious to you;
therefore he will rise up to show you compassion.

ISAIAH 30:18 NIV

If you become so overwhelmed by your own shame, troubles, or misconceptions, you can miss out on the most simple and beautiful truth: God greatly desires to show you grace. When you enter God's presence with this point of view, you are humbled by his love.

What do you need grace for today?

DAY 163

The Comparison Trap

Let each one examine his own work, and then he will have rejoicing in himself alone, and not in another. For each one shall bear his own load.

GALATIANS 6:4-5 NKJV

Comparison is an easy trap to fall into. When you hear someone else share their story, it feels like everything is falling into place exactly as it should. Their life seems far less complicated than yours. Everyone has dark moments. Stop comparing, and give it to God.

What comparison traps do you fall into?

DAY 164

Full Joy

"You also have sorrow now. But I will see you again. Your hearts will rejoice, and no one will take away your joy from you."

JOHN 16:22 CSB

The joy that comes with the presence of God cannot be taken away. When you remember what Christ has done for you, and think about how his grace has changed the eternal course of your life, you cannot help but be filled with an irrepressible joy.

How can you stop your joy from being taken away?

DAY 165

Bold Hope

Since, then, we have such a hope,
we act with great boldness.

2 CORINTHIANS 3:12 CSB

When you fix your eyes on the hope of salvation in Christ Jesus, you cannot help but walk bravely. If a soldier goes into battle already knowing he will come out victorious, he fights with boldness. The battle is already won for you; there is truly nothing to fear.

How can you act with boldness today?

DAY 166

God Searches

"Indeed I Myself will search for My sheep
and seek them out."

EZEKIEL 34:11 NKJV

God values his relationship with you so much that he will go to great lengths to capture your heart. He doesn't just sit, passively waiting for you to approach him. He searches for his sheep. Respond to his pursuit with a heart that is eager to be loved by him.

Have you consciously felt God's pursuit of you?

DAY 167

Portion

"The LORD is my portion," says my soul,
"Therefore I have hope in Him."

LAMENTATIONS 3:24 NASB

This world thrives on consumerism; you are continually encouraged to get more. The stuff of this life will never fill the hunger in your soul. The only proper sustenance for a weary soul is a great God. The Lord is your portion, the perfect portion to fill your emptiness.

How do you make the Lord your portion?

DAY 168

Brought Near

In Christ Jesus you who once were far off have been brought near by the blood of Christ.

Ephesians 2:13 NKJV

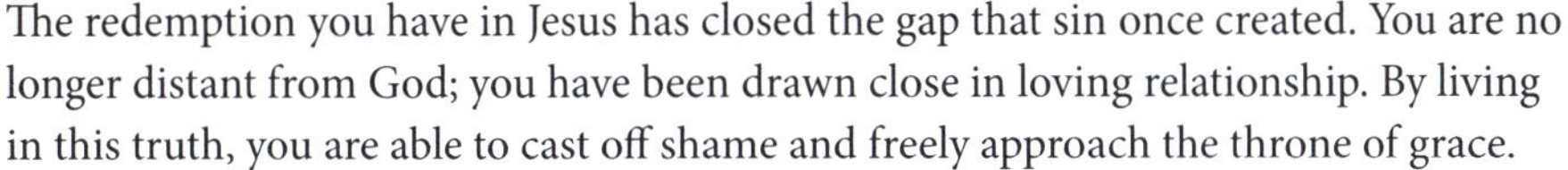

The redemption you have in Jesus has closed the gap that sin once created. You are no longer distant from God; you have been drawn close in loving relationship. By living in this truth, you are able to cast off shame and freely approach the throne of grace.

How often do you approach the throne of grace?

REFLECTIONS OF THE WEEK

DAY 169

Understand and Accept

What you have received is not the spirit of the world, but the Spirit who is from God, so that you may understand what God has freely given us.

1 Corinthians 2:12 NIV

The goodness of God is so far beyond the human capacity for goodness that you may struggle to understand it. This can lead to difficulty in your ability to accept it. But with the Spirit of God in you, you can both comprehend and accept in full what the Father has given.

How do you understand and accept what God has given?

DAY 170

Eternal Legacy

From eternity to eternity
the Lord's faithful love is toward those who fear him.

Psalm 103:17 CSB

By putting your faith in Christ, you have entered into an eternal legacy of faith. With your hope and fear placed in God, you receive his steadfast love and his enduring promise. Rest in the fact that you are loved forever by the perfect lover.

What legacy do you want to leave?

DAY 171

No Reason to Fear

Love the LORD, all you godly ones!
For the LORD protects those who are loyal to him.

PSALM 31:23 NLT

Fear should not be a common emotion for a believer. When you live in the truth that God has already won the victory, there is no reason to be afraid. God never leaves you hopeless and alone. He is by your side through every situation you face.

What fear can you give to God today?

DAY 172

Diligent Seekers

The soul of a lazy man desires, and has nothing;
But the soul of the diligent shall be made rich.

PROVERBS 13:4 NKJV

It is dangerous to become complacent in your Christian walk. When you are content to stay where you are, you will not move forward. In fact, you will likely go backwards. But when you begin to pursue him, you will be propelled forward in your faith.

How can you move forward in your faith?

DAY 173

God's Dwelling Place

Do you not know that you are God's temple
and that God's Spirit dwells in you?

1 Corinthians 3:16 ESV

In the Old Testament, people traveled to the temple and relied on a priest to communicate with God. Upon Christ's death, the curtain separating the holy place was torn, symbolizing the end of separation between God and man. Now the Spirit of God dwells in you. You are the temple.

How do you treat the temple of God?

DAY 174

True Love

"All people will know that you are my followers
if you love each other."

John 13:35 NCV

Love isn't easy. Every human relationship is broken. Love is often about repair. You love past the difficulty and in spite of the inconvenience. True love is patient enough to rise above challenges and seek solutions. It doesn't look to satisfy itself; it gives.

How do you show true love?

DAY 175

Commissioned to Boldness

"As Moses lifted up the serpent in the wilderness, even so must the Son of Man be lifted up; so that whoever believes will in Him have eternal life."

JOHN 3:14-15 NASB

Moses complied even with God's most awkward, uncomfortable commands. You have a commission similar to Moses': lift Jesus high and tell people to look to him for eternal life. It may seem awkward, but you have to set that feeling aside. Be bold and share God's love.

How can you be bold with God's commands?

REFLECTIONS OF THE WEEK

DAY 176

In the Race

"Do not be afraid; you have done all this evil. Yet do not turn aside from following the LORD, but serve the LORD with all your heart."

1 SAMUEL 12:20 ESV

You may struggle, thinking you need to forgive yourself because you lack peace about the sins of your past. The fact of the matter is this: Jesus has set you free, so you have no opinion in the matter any longer. Get up and run again.

How can you serve the Lord with all your heart?

DAY 177

Remember God's Faithfulness

Because he has his heart set on me, I will deliver him;
I will protect him because he knows my name.

PSALM 91:14 CSB

When you read God's Word, you glue your need to God's provision. Whether it's for love or wisdom, provision or righteousness, Jesus has all you need. He is a generous giver, and he has beckoned you closer to receive what he has for you.

What do you need God to provide for you today?

DAY 178

Strength Every Morning

Be our strength every morning,
our salvation in time of distress.

Isaiah 33:2 NIV

In times of crisis, each new morning demands your strength. In seasons of difficulty, waking may bring with it worry or fear. Christ is the ultimate source of strength. Open his Word each morning and counteract worry with peace and fear with understanding.

How can you make God your first source?

DAY 179

Unless the Lord

Unless the Lord builds a house,
the work of the builders is wasted.

Psalm 127:1 NLT

To attempt any great work apart from Christ is meaningless. Without seeking to work alongside him, your efforts are wasted, and your goals are futile. When you choose to partner with Almighty God in the work he is already doing, you experience the joy of his blessing.

How do you let God build your house?

DAY 180

Goodness in Waiting

The LORD is good to those who wait for him,
to the person who seeks him.

LAMENTATIONS 3:25 CSB

Have you ever watched other people enjoy their "happily-ever-afters" while you sat wondering if yours would ever come? Waiting is challenging enough without watching everyone else rush ahead of you. But God promises goodness to those who wait.

How good are you at waiting?

DAY 181

Grit of Grace

Don't pay attention to everything people say, or you may hear your servant cursing you, for you know that many times you yourself have cursed others.

ECCLESIASTES 7:21-22 NCV

There is something awful about hearing someone has spoken badly about you behind your back. You want a chance to defend yourself. Instead of quickly becoming angry, consider your own failings. This is how you come face-to-face with the grit of grace.

How hard is it for you to extend grace?

DAY 182

Simply Listen

After the earthquake, there was a fire, but the LORD was not in the fire.
After the fire, there was a quiet, gentle sound.

1 KINGS 19:12 NCV

Hurricanes, earthquakes, and tornadoes are sometimes referred to as acts of God, but that expression can lead us to misunderstand God and how he works. Sometimes he is found in a simple whisper. Look past the fires that command your attention, and simply listen.

How do you hear God's voice?

REFLECTIONS OF THE WEEK

DAY 183

A Generous Heart

A generous person will prosper;
whoever refreshes others will be refreshed.

PROVERBS 11:25 NIV

On the surface, this verse may seem to suggest that you give in order to get. Looking deeper, you see beyond. Giving is an act; generosity is a condition of the heart. Only a generous heart is refreshed by giving. It is this generous heart your Father waits eagerly to bless.

How can you be generous today?

DAY 184

A Sure Foundation

In that day he will be your sure foundation,
providing a rich store of salvation, wisdom, and knowledge.

ISAIAH 33:6 NLT

Whether from physical danger or emotional insecurity, you need never allow fear to take hold of you. Once you have been saved by God's grace, once you know him and understand the foundation on which you stand, no power on earth can shake you.

How sure is your foundation?

DAY 185

Truly Free

Out of my distress I called on the LORD;
the LORD answered me and set me free.

PSALM 118:5 ESV

Consider what your freedom really means as an adopted child of the Almighty. He has chosen to call you his, and that means you can be set free from fear, sin, and death! Just calling him Father gives you more freedom than some will ever know.

How can you share this incredible truth?

DAY 186

For His Glory

"I will do whatever you ask in my name,
so that the Father may be glorified in the Son."

JOHN 14:13 NIV

How do you reconcile this incredible truth with seemingly unanswered prayers? He promises to do whatever you ask in his name, in order to glorify the Father. Jesus sees well past today. Perhaps to bring glory to God you sometimes need a different answer than you hoped for.

How does this resonate with you?

DAY 187

No Plan B

My victory and honor come from God alone.
He is my refuge, a rock where no enemy can reach me.

Psalm 62:7 NLT

In matters of faith, God is the single source of your safety, your only means to victory. The good news: if you are truly his, you don't need a Plan B. His love, plan, and provision are all you need. Resist the desire to control things yourself and rest in the safety of his arms.

What Plan B have you entertained?

DAY 188

In the Light

With You is the fountain of life;
In Your light we see light.

Psalm 36:9 NKJV

How would you explain color to a blind person? What is blue, and what makes it unique from red, purple, or green? In order to understand pink, you need to have experienced it. It is the same with goodness, love, and light.

How well do you know the light?

DAY 189

Peace Is Mine

May the Lord of peace himself give you peace
at all times in every way.

2 THESSALONIANS 3:16 ESV

Think of a time when your life was absolutely perfect. Whether for a moment or a minute, eventually real life crept back in. Here on earth, things will never be perfect. This is why the peace of God is so valuable! It forms a barrier between you and things that steal your joy.

When do you experience the most peace?

REFLECTIONS OF THE WEEK

REFLECTIONS

REFLECTIONS

DAY 190

Best Day Ever

A single day in your courts
is better than a thousand anywhere else!

PSALM 84:10 NLT

How many ordinary days would a day in God's presence be worth? Would you rather be poor but surrounded by people full of love and integrity, or wealthy living among those who compromise morality and goodness?

How does your life reflect your desire for God?

DAY 191

Privilege of Suffering

It has been granted to you on Christ's behalf not only to believe in him,
but also to suffer for him.

PHILIPPIANS 1:29 CSB

By its very definition, suffering is not enjoyable. Yet it is supposed to be a blessing, or something to be desired, if done for Christ? Consider what he suffered for you. To experience pain while pursuing him is to know more of his heart. That is a privilege.

What suffering do you experience?

DAY 192

Perfect Peace

You will keep in perfect peace all who trust in you,
all whose thoughts are fixed on you!

ISAIAH 26:3 NLT

What robs you of your peace? These words in Isaiah are not a bargain. They are an observation. When you trust God fully, and keep your mind on him, you naturally feel peace. Thoughts fixed on him are thoughts steeped in tranquility.

Do you think of peace as a reward or an outcome?

DAY 193

Arm to Lean On

The everlasting God is your place of safety,
and his arms will hold you up forever.

DEUTERONOMY 33:27 NCV

In comedy, it's not uncommon to see a character lean against an unstable surface and realize they misplaced their trust. What looked like a wall was not. Arms flail, legs fly, you laugh. It's less funny when you're the one flailing. God is your only true source of stability. Lean on him!

How do you depend on God?

DAY 194

Like a Child

"Truly I tell you, anyone who will not receive the kingdom of God like a little child will never enter it."

MARK 10:15 NIV

Picture Christmas morning: children running down the stairs, tearing gleefully into packages. Every gift brings fresh exclamations of gratitude and joy. Receiving the kingdom of God should be like this! Be filled with wonder, enthusiasm, and thanks.

How is this working in your life?

DAY 195

By His Wounds

The punishment that brought us peace was on him, and by his wounds you are healed.

ISAIAH 53:5 NIV

Seldom do you feel more loved than when someone has suffered for you. No amount of suffering could be a fair exchange for all the world's sin, yet Jesus' pain was essential. Why? So you would feel the weight of your sin, and the weight of his great, great love.

Do you feel the weight of his love?

DAY 196

Renewal

You were dead because of your sins.... Then God made you alive with Christ, for he forgave all your sins.

COLOSSIANS 2:13 NLT

As long as you are here, you'll face temptation from the world. Renewal is an ongoing process. Each time you find yourself conforming, you must re-transform, renew. What a blessing it is to know that you can. Again and again, he welcomes you.

How can you transform your mind?

REFLECTIONS OF THE WEEK

DAY 197

Openly and Utterly

"Let the little children come to me, and do not hinder them, for the kingdom of God belongs to such as these."

MARK 10:14 NIV

Jesus loved children. The Bible doesn't have many stories of him with children, but the ones listed make it clear: he found them incredibly special. Why? Children have a way of being. Authenticity. Maybe their absolute dependence was what captivated his heart.

How can you become more like a child?

DAY 198

Start Here

The beginning of wisdom is this: Get wisdom. Though it cost all you have, get understanding.

PROVERBS 4:7 NIV

The first step on the path to wisdom? Realize how vital it is. Understanding is worth everything you have. According to this verse, nothing matters more. No matter how successful or happy you are, if you don't "get it," you will be missing out.

What can you do to acquire wisdom?

DAY 199

Astounding Love

The LORD put a mark on Cain to warn
anyone who might try to kill him.

GENESIS 4:15 NLT

God's love and his capacity to forgive knows no boundaries. Anyone killing Cain could expect a punishment seven times more severe than the one Cain himself received. This protection showed God's incredible love. And this is the God you serve!

When are you astounded by God's love?

DAY 200

Joyful in Tribulation

I am filled with comfort.
I am exceedingly joyful in all your tribulation.

2 CORINTHIANS 7:4 NKJV

What would it take to be joyful in prison? Can you honestly imagine it? On your own, it would be impossible. But you are not alone. Joy is happiness regardless of circumstances and untouchable peace. It was Paul's, and it can be yours.

What does exceeding joy look like to you?

DAY 201

Seek His Face

Seek the Lord and His strength;
Seek His face continually.

Psalm 105:4 NASB

God desires more than presence and conversation. He wants intimacy. "Seek my face," he says. He wants you to pursue him for more than forgiveness and answered prayer. Nothing matters more than seeking the face of God. In his presence, all is well.

How do you seek the Lord?

DAY 202

Totally Committed

The Lord is faithful; he will strengthen you
and guard you from the evil one.

2 Thessalonians 3:3 NLT

Faithful friends never betray you. A faithful dog sticks close to your side. A faithful spouse has eyes only for you. The Lord is faithful. Allow this incredible truth to strengthen and sustain you as you face whatever happens today. God will never betray you.

How have you seen God's faithfulness?

DAY 203

Under His Arm

Let all who take refuge in you be glad;
let them ever sing for joy.

PSALM 5:11 NIV

Summer heat sometimes brings summer storms. With a tornado heading your way, you'd seek protection. You'd get low, beneath something sturdy and strong. The Lord wants to be your shelter from the storms of life. Take refuge under his strong arms.

Are you glad that God is your refuge?

REFLECTIONS OF THE WEEK

DAY 204

Abiding Love

Satisfy us in the morning with your unfailing love,
that you may sing for joy and be glad all your days.

PSALM 90:14 NIV

Think of brand-new love, where the newness and the enthusiasm are almost overwhelming. Whether a romance, a new pet, or even a new fitness plan, that feeling may or may not take root. A relationship with Jesus brings satisfaction and joy forever!

Has discovering God given way to deeper joy?

DAY 205

Naked and Exposed

Nothing in all creation is hidden from God.
Everything is naked and exposed before his eyes.

HEBREWS 4:13 NLT

There is absolutely nothing about you that God doesn't see and doesn't know, and he finds you every bit as precious as a baby in a bathtub. His love is incomprehensible, and his grace is relentless. You don't have to hide from him.

How vulnerable are you with God?

DAY 206

Friendship

Do not forsake your friend or a friend of your family…
better a neighbor nearby than a relative far away.

PROVERBS 27:10 NIV

The Bible makes it clear you are meant to have friends. These are the people who are with you simply because you are you. Loving, committed friendship is God's plan—and his gift. Take care to nurture those relationships and be the kind of friend others seek out in a time of need.

What friend can you appreciate today?

DAY 207

Heart-longing

My heart said of you, "Go, worship him."
So I come to worship you, LORD.

PSALM 27:8 NCV

When struggling with an important decision, you're often advised to listen to your heart. If the Holy Spirit is an active part of your life, your heart will be directed toward God. In times of need, in times of joy, listen to your heart and worship your God.

How have you listened to your heart lately?

DAY 208

Home

"I will come back and take you to be with me
that you also may be where I am."

JOHN 14:3 NIV

Where is home? For some, the place they came from will always be home. Others have found or created it in a new place of their own choosing. Maybe it isn't even a place, but a feeling you get with certain people. Your true and perfect home is in heaven with God.

How can you make God your home?

DAY 209

Lost and Found

I have gone astray like a lost sheep; seek Your servant,
For I do not forget Your commandments.

PSALM 119:176 NASB

GPS and smart phones have made it more rare, but occasionally, you may be lost. With no familiar landmarks and no one to follow, your only option is to ask for help. Don't lose sight of the route on your faith walk. Call for help when you start to feel lost.

Who do you call when you feel lost?

DAY 210

He Is Watching

The LORD will watch over your coming and going
both now and forevermore.

PSALM 121:8 NIV

When you take a small child to a park, both danger and delight are everywhere. You know not to take your eyes off that child. In the same way, God never stops watching you. You will experience life's ups and downs. Know that because he is with you, you'll be okay.

Can you sense God watching you?

REFLECTIONS OF THE WEEK

DAY 211

As I Should Be

There is surely a future hope for you,
and your hope will not be cut off.

PROVERBS 23:18 NIV

God made you carefully and intentionally. He knew exactly what he was doing and why. Even the desires of your heart are there to lead to the Father's plan for your life. The next time you doubt your worth, remember these words.

What wonderful things did God prepare in advance for you to do?

DAY 212

All for Good

"You intended to harm me, but God intended it all for good.
He brought me to this position so I could save the lives of many people."

GENESIS 50:20 NLT

Even in the wake of unspeakable tragedy, God can lead you through it. He holds you close, and shapes you into who you're meant to be. Within God's perfect plan, even other people's sins against you can be used for good. Look to God to make everything beautiful.

What good can you see in your difficult situation?

DAY 213

Look to the Mountains

I lift up my eyes to the mountains—
where does my help come from?

PSALM 121:1 NIV

It's easy to look somewhere other than God for help. When someone is desperate, they search frantically. True help comes from the Lord. He's the maker of the entire universe. Don't look to the created; look to the Creator. You will not be left wanting.

Where do you look when you're desperate?

DAY 214

Seek and Find

"Keep on asking, and you will receive what you ask for. Keep on seeking, and you will find. Keep on knocking, and the door will be opened to you."

LUKE 11:9 NLT

Few treasure hunts will guarantee any return on your dollar or your time. There is one treasure hunt you can guarantee will leave you fulfilled. Seek God and you will find him. He promises this in his Word. Any investment you make in seeking him will be rewarded.

What are you seeking?

DAY 215

Casting

Cast all your anxiety on him
because he cares for you.

1 Peter 5:7 NIV

Have you ever been anxious or paralyzed with fear? What should you do as God's child? His advice is simple. Cast it to him. When you cast anxiety instead of holding it, you will enjoy abundant freedom.

How can you start a habit of casting?

DAY 216

Delivered from Fear

I sought the Lord, and he answered me
and delivered me from all my fears.

Psalm 34:4 ESV

When seeds of fear sink into your heart, they can grow into giant trees of debilitating behaviors that paralyze you. You have an advocate who has the power to demolish every stronghold and fear that has ever gripped you! Call out to God, and he will answer you.

What fear can you release to God today?

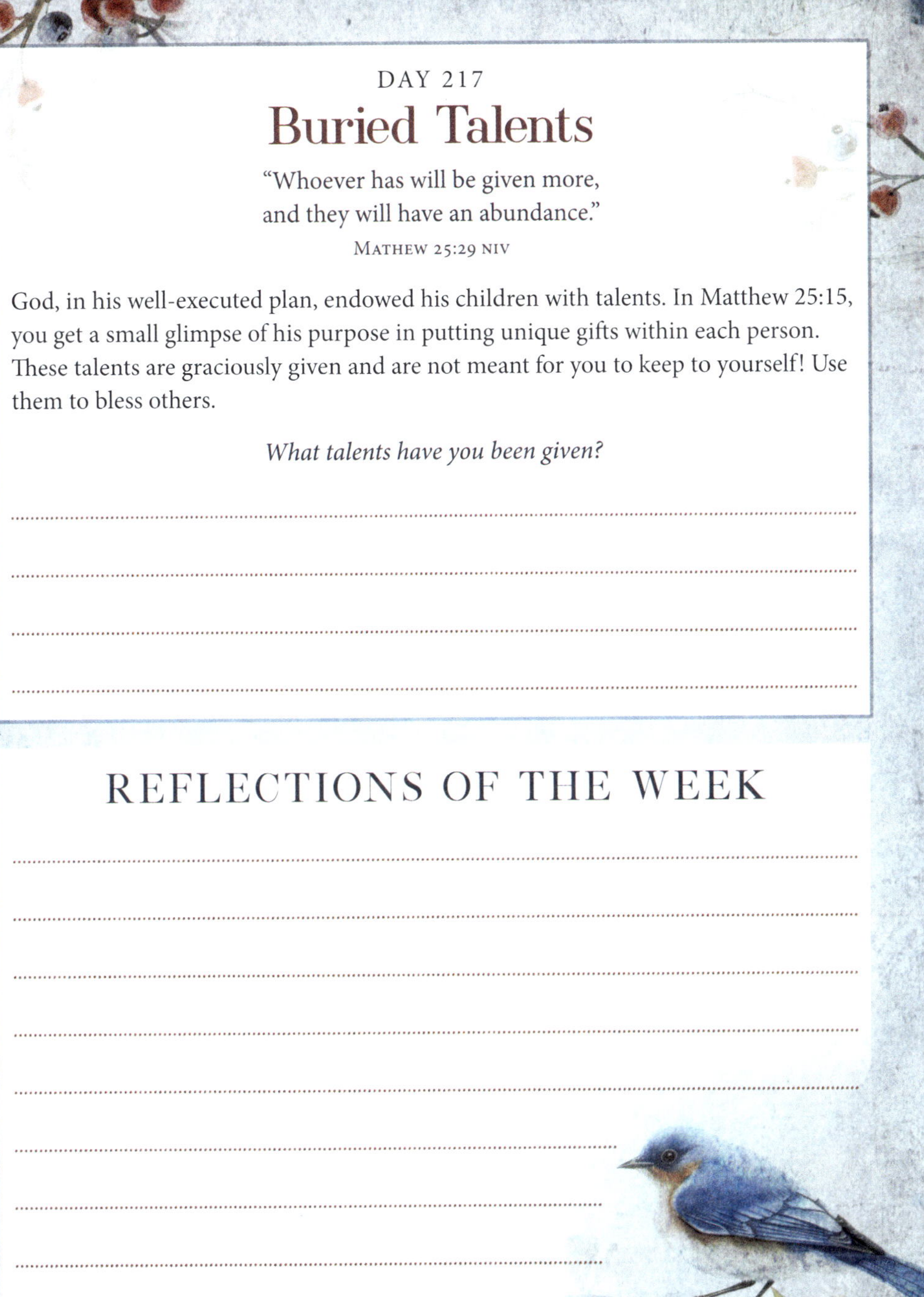

DAY 217

Buried Talents

"Whoever has will be given more,
and they will have an abundance."

MATHEW 25:29 NIV

God, in his well-executed plan, endowed his children with talents. In Matthew 25:15, you get a small glimpse of his purpose in putting unique gifts within each person. These talents are graciously given and are not meant for you to keep to yourself! Use them to bless others.

What talents have you been given?

REFLECTIONS OF THE WEEK

DAY 218

Thorns

In order to keep me from becoming conceited, I was given a thorn in my flesh... Three times I pleaded with the Lord to take it away from me.

2 Corinthians 12:7-8 NIV

Every child of God is profoundly imperfect. Many weaknesses can be managed and some can be healed. But rest assured, they will not go away altogether. Remaining weak means you can be strong in him. Remain in the place of humility and cling to God for strength and comfort.

What is your thorn?

DAY 219

True Strength

I pray that from his glorious, unlimited resources he will empower you with inner strength through his Spirit.

Ephesians 3:16 NLT

God has not asked you to be strong. He did make you to be a model of his strength though. There is a big difference between being strong in your own power and being strong in God's power. He has unlimited resources for you to tap into!

How do you display God's strength?

DAY 220

Pouring

In the last days I will pour out my Spirit
on all kinds of people.

ACTS 2:17 NCV

Did you pour anything this morning? Milk on cereal, water on plants, creamer in coffee, or bathwater on a child's head? Pouring is very different than dripping. It is an unleashing that saturates. God knows that you don't just need a trickle or a sprinkling of his Spirit.

When was the last time you felt drenched in the Spirit?

DAY 221

Hearing Truth

"When he, the Spirit of truth, comes,
he will guide you into all truth."

JOHN 16:13 NIV

The world will not counsel you in the ways of God. It will urge you to hate your body, hold a grudge, and accept every sin. These messages will be spoken loudly. It is of utmost importance to regularly hear, read, and meditate on the truth found in God's Word.

Where do you get your truth?

DAY 222

An Anchored Soul

Then you will experience God's peace.... His peace will guard
your hearts and minds as you live in Christ Jesus.

PHILIPPIANS 4:7 NLT

No matter how uncertain your future may be, or how confusing your circumstances, your life is firmly established on the faithfulness of God. Nothing can shake you when your eternity is secure. No matter what you face, your hope can be anchored in God.

What are you anchored to?

DAY 223

Finishing Touches

Looking unto Jesus, the author and
finisher of your faith.

HEBREWS 12:2 NKJV

Have you ever watched an artist paint a picture? He begins with an unblemished white canvas. In the last few moments, he applies the fine detail and extra colors that make the painting truly complete. Don't walk away before God is finished creating a masterpiece out of you!

What is God working on in you now?

DAY 224

Just Run

Since we also have such a large cloud of witnesses surrounding us, let us lay aside every hindrance and the sin that so easily ensnares us.

HEBREWS 12:1 CSB

The nature of sin is to cling. Like a dryer sheet stuck to a sweater, sin sticks, and it won't simply fall off you. It takes an intentional action to remove or resist it. But it can be conquered. If you are casually swiping away the sin in your life, perhaps it's time for a different approach.

How do you run away from sin?

REFLECTIONS OF THE WEEK

DAY 225

Divine Citizenship

He has granted to us his precious and very great promises,
so that through them you may become partakers of the divine nature.

2 PETER 1:4 ESV

If you have given your life to God, you have become a citizen of his kingdom. No one knows what will happen around the globe in the next 100 years. There might be much more shaking to come. If your hope isn't set on your earthly nation, you will be okay.

Where is your citizenship?

DAY 226

The Gift of Song

Praise the LORD!
Sing to the LORD a new song.

PSALM 149:1 ESV

Some people are singers and some aren't. Regardless of which camp you land in, God has still given you the gift of song. Singing to God is an act of worship that he delights in regardless of your vocal ability. Sing something new from your heart to his!

What song is in your heart?

DAY 227

Parental Words

You are precious in my eyes,
and honored, and I love you.

Isaiah 43:4 ESV

Parental words carry power. They may have helped you face your greatest fears, or they could have whispered lies of defeat. God's voice carries more weight and power than anyone else's. As his child, you can receive his words of love and life.

What parental words do you hear?

DAY 228

Washed Away

"Already you are clean because of the word
that I have spoken to you."

John 15:3 ESV

Have you ever had a stain on a shirt that wouldn't come out? After you tried everything, you had to accept the fact that the stain was there to stay. The stain of sin can only be removed by the work of Christ on the cross. Confess it to him, and you will be clean!

What do you want to be clean from?

DAY 229

Trouble

The righteous person faces many troubles,
but the LORD comes to the rescue each time.

PSALM 34:19 NLT

Knowing exactly what his disciples needed to hear before he died, Jesus gave a lot of counsel. He wanted to make sure their theology accepted that, even in the life of a believer, suffering would be present. It is simply part of living here on earth. God has not and will not leave you.

What trouble are you facing?

DAY 230

Not of This World

"My kingdom does not belong to this world."

JOHN 18:36 NCV

If you consume a regular diet of nightly news, it might be easy for you to become depressed. Wickedness seems to prevail. God's kingdom won't be fully expressed here on earth. He is building one that cannot be shaken. It will never end!

What do you think God's kingdom looks like?

DAY 231

In the Love

Keep yourselves in God's love as you wait for the Lord Jesus Christ with his mercy to give you life forever.

JUDE 1:21 NCV

What does it mean to keep yourself in God's love? You may be tempted to leave when you face hardship. Nothing delights God more than a heart of faith that says, "Despite what I might see or experience, I still believe that you are a God of love."

How do you remain in God's love?

REFLECTIONS OF THE WEEK

DAY 232

Becoming Childlike

"Truly I tell you, unless you change and become like little children,
you will never enter the kingdom of heaven."

MATTHEW 18:3 NIV

Much of your childhood is spent preparing to be an adult. It wouldn't be right to remain a child. In your spiritual journey, though, it's the opposite. Become like a child. Resist proud, adult-like tendencies and happily submit to God's leadership and provision.

How can you practice being like a child?

DAY 233

Not Worth Comparing

I consider that your present sufferings are not worth comparing
with the glory that will be revealed in us.

ROMANS 8:18 NIV

The disciples who walked with Jesus all suffered: some as martyrs unto death, some watching their loved ones die, and others being shunned. The glory of God's coming kingdom will be so amazing that your trials will pale in comparison. Find courage to keep pressing on.

How do you view suffering?

DAY 234

Rejoice in Suffering

We can rejoice, too, when we run into problems and trials,
for we know that they help us develop endurance.

ROMANS 5:3 NLT

There is more to do in your sufferings than suffer. God says you can rejoice. Suffering produces something good: endurance. Endurance grows through trial and tribulation—not when things are easy. It's what allows you to go further. Press on!

How does suffering develop endurance in you?

DAY 235

Feeding on Faithfulness

Trust in the Lord, and do good;
Dwell in the land, and feed on His faithfulness.

PSALM 37:3 NKJV

The person who trusts in the Lord has a beautiful life. Trust alleviates all the natural tensions. You can be at peace knowing God will faithfully care for all your needs. Do what is good in the land, rest in Christ, and enjoy the faithfulness of your heavenly Father.

What does trust look like for you?

DAY 236

Not without Hope

We were given this hope
when we were saved.

Romans 8:24 NLT

When you chose to trust God with your life, you did it in hope. You hoped that your new life would be better than your present one. You hoped that he would take your life and use it for his glory. And you continue to hope that you will see him face to face one day.

What is your hope?

DAY 237

Continual Intercession

Christ Jesus died, but he was also raised from the dead,
and now he is on God's right side, appealing to God for us.

Romans 8:34 NCV

Some of the most comforting words a child can ever hear are a parent's prayers. Perhaps your earthly parents aren't praying. Take heart. There is still one who is. Jesus has the Father's ear, and he is continually making intercession for you. Your name is written on his hand.

What do you want Jesus to pray for?

DAY 238

Strong Faith

Faith comes from what is heard, and what is heard
comes through the message about Christ.

ROMANS 10:17 CSB

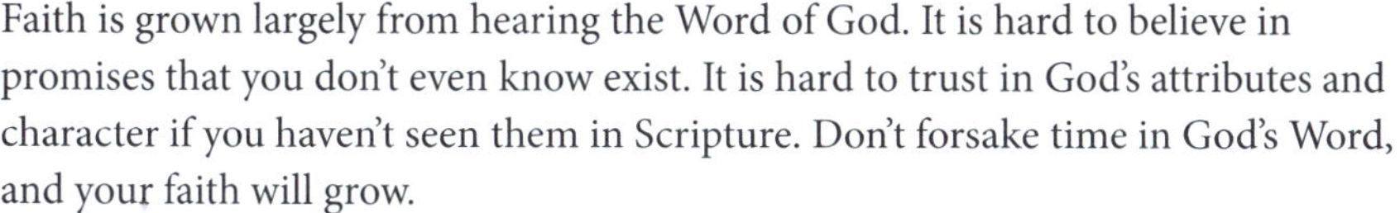

Faith is grown largely from hearing the Word of God. It is hard to believe in promises that you don't even know exist. It is hard to trust in God's attributes and character if you haven't seen them in Scripture. Don't forsake time in God's Word, and your faith will grow.

How do you build your faith?

REFLECTIONS OF THE WEEK

DAY 239

Near

The Lord is near to the brokenhearted;
he saves those crushed in spirit.

Psalm 34:18 CSB

Being brokenhearted is no small thing. It is not mere discouragement; it is severe pain that is hard to bounce back from. There is little that can be done. But there is one who is fully equipped to bear your pain. He is already nearer than you realize.

Does God feel near to you today?

DAY 240

Superhuman Expectations

May he give you the power to accomplish all the good things
your faith prompts you to do.

2 Thessalonians 1:11 NLT

Perhaps there are expectations placed on you that are unreasonable. Don't exhaust yourself trying to be someone you can't be. God isn't asking you to be superhuman. He knows your frame. He is your maker and your designer. Draw your strength from him.

What superhuman expectations are you under?

DAY 241

Steadfast Love

As high as the heavens are above the earth,
so great is his steadfast love toward those who fear him.

Psalm 103:11 ESV

Take a moment to contemplate steadfast love. It doesn't get offended easily. It can weather incredible relational strain. It can handle faithlessness. It won't quit even when the recipient's love has grown cold. This is how God describes his love toward his children.

How have you encountered the steadfast love of God?

DAY 242

Worthless Things

Turn my eyes from looking at worthless things;
and give me life in your ways.

Psalm 119:37 ESV

There is no doubt that social media can be both a gift and a colossal waste of time. There are worthless things all over social media outlets. You are not alone in your struggle to resist it. God wants you to have life, and that comes as you walk in his ways.

How can you turn away from worthless things?

DAY 243

Growing Weary

Let us not grow weary of doing good, for in due season you will reap, if you do not give up.

GALATIANS 6:9 ESV

A time-tested principle is that you reap what you sow. Apart from any environmental upheaval, if you plant corn, you will reap corn. The same principle applies to sowing seeds of goodness. If you sow forgiveness, gentleness, and honesty, you will reap the fruit of those seeds.

What seeds are you sowing?

DAY 244

A Basket Case

"I took the load off their shoulders;
I let them put down their baskets."

PSALM 81:6 NCV

Physical burdens require strength and stamina. Spiritual and emotional burdens are the same. You have a burden bearer. Put all of your concerns, worries, fears, and doubts into God's mighty basket and let him haul it away! You don't have to be a basket case!

What baskets can you put down today?

DAY 245

Shining

"You are the light of the world.
A city set on a hill cannot be hidden."

MATTHEW 5:14 ESV

Lights from major cities can be seen from space. They simply cannot be hidden. As a believer, you can be a light, shining for all to see. Don't hide behind the façade of political correctness and fear, but rather speak and live in the luminance of Christ's truth.

How do you shine for all to see?

REFLECTIONS OF THE WEEK

DAY 246

Bad News

They will have no fear of bad news;
their hearts are steadfast, trusting in the Lord.

PSALM 112:7 NIV

In this age of technology, you can be inundated with happenings from around the world. You do not have to fear bad news! If your heart is righteous, you are steadfast and secure. In spite of alarming information, you can be at peace because you are safe in God's hands.

What is your typical response to bad news?

DAY 247

Bloom

"They are those who, hearing the word, hold it fast in an
honest and good heart, and bear fruit with patience."

LUKE 8:15 ESV

It's comforting to believe that the routine of your ordinary life is merely preparation for the really big assignment that surely is coming. Then one day in a moment of quiet, the Lord whispers, "This is it. This is what I've called you to do. Be faithful right where I've put you."

How can you bloom in the ordinary?

DAY 248

Prowling Lion

Stay alert! Watch out for your great enemy, the devil. He prowls around like a roaring lion, looking for someone to devour.

1 PETER 5:8-9 NLT

A lion that roars is not to be feared because he has given his presence away, allowing his prey time to escape. When you are in tune with God, you don't need to fear Satan's tactics. You will hear the roar a mile away and take appropriate action to see to his defeat.

Are you in tune with God?

DAY 249

Bridging the Gap

Faith is the confidence that what you hope for will actually happen; it gives us assurance about things you cannot see.

HEBREWS 11:1 NLT

Do you ever feel like there is an enormous gap between what you know to be true in God's Word and what you feel to be true? How do you move from the tyranny of emotions to the confidence of faith? Determine to believe what God says instead of what your emotions say.

How can you believe God over your emotions?

DAY 250

Only Dust

For He Himself knows your frame;
He is mindful that you are but dust.

PSALM 103:14 NASB

You are incredibly important dust to God. He knows your frame because he framed you! He knows you are weak, and without his powerful hand upon you, you would be irrecoverably destroyed. But one day, your body of dust will be exchanged for a glorious eternal one!

How do you feel about getting a new body?

DAY 251

Clay Pots

We are the clay, you are the potter;
we are all the work of your hand.

ISAIAH 64:8 NIV

God uses this imagery all the way from Genesis to Revelation. He is the potter; you are the clay. He has power to create exactly according to his wish; the pot has no say. But the vessel itself is not what gives it worth. The value lies in the contents.

How has God been shaping you?

DAY 252

Eat for Life

Man does not live by bread alone, but man lives by everything that proceeds out of the mouth of the LORD.

DEUTERONOMY 8:3 NASB

The Scriptures are your spiritual food: a veritable banquet laid out for your enjoyment. The Word will nourish, guide, comfort, convict, and satisfy every hungry and thirsty soul. Read it and remember that it nourishes, strengthens, and gives you tools for life.

Do you live by the Word of God?

REFLECTIONS OF THE WEEK

REFLECTIONS

REFLECTIONS

DAY 253

Necessary Instrument

All Scripture is inspired by God and profitable… so that the man of God may be adequate, equipped for every good work.

2 TIMOTHY 3:16-17 NASB

Most tasks require a tool. It may be a broom, drill, lawnmower, hose, bucket, hammer, or parachute! It takes something to accomplish something. You need tools for your spiritual life as well. Don't struggle along without the necessary instrument for success—the Bible.

How do you make the Bible your instrument?

DAY 254

Faith's End

"If you have faith like a grain of mustard seed, you will say to this mountain, 'Move from here to there,' and it will move."

MATTHEW 17:20 ESV

Trusting God is not always easy. It means you are at peace with any outcome. You might pray earnestly for a specific answer, and you think the outcome of that prayer reveals the measure of your faith. But the end result of your faith is the salvation of your soul!

How has faith led to your salvation?

DAY 255

Held Together

He is before all things,
and in him all things hold together.

COLOSSIANS 1:17 NIV

Life sometimes seems to be a conglomeration of unrelated activities, and you feel pulled in a thousand directions simultaneously. Frustration, discouragement, and anxiety often overwhelm. It is not your job to hold your life together. Submit to God as the glue.

How has God held you together?

DAY 256

How You Love

This is love: that you walk in obedience to his commands. As you have heard from the beginning, his command is that you walk in love.

2 JOHN 6 NIV

Love is probably the most overused, over romanticized word in the human language. You fall in love, you love pizza, and you love your dog. But how do you love an invisible being? Don't search for an elusive emotion. The proof of your love for God is your obedience.

How do you love God?

DAY 257

Idols of the Heart

"These leaders have set up idols in their hearts....
Why should I listen to their requests?"

EZEKIEL 14:3 NLT

Whatever consumes your time could become an idol of the heart. Maybe it's time do to some soul searching. What squanders your time, your thoughts, and dictates your priorities? Are you embracing things that will lead you into sin?

What is consuming your time?

DAY 258

Joy

Do not grieve, for the joy of the LORD
is your strength.

NEHEMIAH 8:10 NIV

Happiness is dependent on circumstances; joy is not. Happiness is fleeting; joy is constant. Happiness disappears when trials come; joy grows through troubles. It can't be faked. It's expressed in song, laughter, and a serenity that belies any adversity. Joy is found in God alone.

How is joy present in your life?

DAY 259

Kept

Anyone born of God does not continue to sin; the One who was born of God keeps them safe, and the evil one cannot harm them.

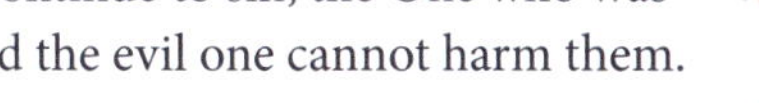

1 JOHN 5:1 NIV

God's Word is clear about what he expects of us. His purpose is to keep us from harm. If you have submitted yourself to God, you will obey. God's involvement with your obedience is profound. He not only gives you the strength but the will to obey him!

Do you find it easy to obey God?

REFLECTIONS OF THE WEEK

DAY 260

End of the Tunnel

"I am the light of the world. Whoever follows me will
never walk in darkness, but will have the light of life."

John 8:12 NIV

"There is a light at the end of the tunnel." There may be times when there is no positive ending. What then? Jesus is light and he dwells in you. You are surrounded by his presence no matter where you are. Walk through your tunnels blazing with the light of Jesus!

What tunnel of yours needs light?

DAY 261

Never Give Up

I call on you, my God, for you will answer me;
turn your ear to me and hear my prayer.

Psalm 17:6 NIV

Jesus taught that you should pray and never give up. God will never put you off or turn you away. Many times he waits to answer for a variety of reasons. Perhaps the most important reason is that in the waiting, you will learn to seek him.

How do you hold on to the promise that God will answer you?

DAY 262

Perennials

As the soil makes the sprout come up…
so the Sovereign Lord will make righteousness and praise spring up.

ISAIAH 61:11 NIV

Some perennials are garden bullies. If you're not careful, your entire garden can be overrun by them. There are things in life that may not be wrong in themselves, but when they are allowed to take over, they become a huge detriment to your spiritual growth. Weed them out!

How can you make sure righteousness grows in you?

DAY 263

Sins of Omission

To one who knows the right thing to do and
does not do it, to him it is sin.

JAMES 4:17 NASB

Sins of commission are fairly obvious; those of omission are easier to rationalize away. The Holy Spirit prompts you, but if you're too consumed by your own plans, you might miss it. Make sure you take time to heed the gentle voice of the Holy Spirit.

What has the Holy Spirit been asking you to do?

DAY 264

Starting Over

Oh, give thanks to the LORD, for He is good!
For His mercy endures forever.

PSALM 106:1 NKJV

God says you can start over every morning because his mercies will be there. Whatever went awry the day before, whatever mess you made, you can begin the next day with a completely clean slate! Your part in the transaction is easy: repent and move on.

What do you need God's mercy for today?

DAY 265

The Deliverance Trilogy

He has delivered us from such a deadly peril, and he will deliver us again.
On him we have set our hope that he will continue to deliver us.

2 CORINTHIANS 1:10 NIV

Deliverance. What a marvelous word. Bound by sin, you were delivered. Battling temptation and faltering faith, you were delivered again. As adversity finds your doorstep again, you have the hope that God will continue to deliver you. It's a trilogy of deliverance—freedom!

Do you see the pattern of deliverance in your life?

DAY 266

Divine Song

Shout with joy to the LORD, all the earth;
burst into songs and make music.

PSALM 98:4 NCV

The gift of music is surely from the heart of God. Melodies, harmonies, rhythms, and the infinite configuration of notes and styles inspire, soothe, and stimulate. Mortal music is a wonder. But God sings over you with melodies of victory! You are cocooned in the divine song.

What song can you bring to God today?

REFLECTIONS OF THE WEEK

DAY 267

The Vine

"I am the vine, you are the branches; he who abides in Me and I in him, he bears much fruit, for apart from Me you can do nothing."

JOHN 15:5 NASB

Jesus is the vine. His people are the branches that must remain in him to receive sustenance. If you are attached to anything other than Jesus, you will wither away and die. Without the life of the vine flowing through you, you will bear no fruit. Stay connected to the vine!

How do you stay connected to Jesus?

DAY 268

Absolute Truth

We know that you belong to God.... And your lives are in the True One and in his Son, Jesus Christ. He is the true God and the eternal life.

1 JOHN 5:19-20 NCV

Grey areas have emerged where black and white should be. John clearly states that you can know absolute truth. God keeps you safe from sin and the evil one, you belong to God, and you can know the True One. It's all right there in God's Word.

How can you cling to the truth?

DAY 269

Unchanging

Jesus Christ is the same yesterday
and today and forever.

HEBREWS 13:8 NASB

The word *change* itself can evoke a number of negative responses. There is safety in the familiar. Relationships change, friends move, loved ones pass on, culture shifts, and it can be painful. God's Word contains the one assurance you need: God never changes.

How do you handle change?

DAY 270

Waiting

Wait for the LORD;
Be strong, and let your heart take courage.

PSALM 27:14 NASB

Is there anything positive to be said about waiting? It seems like a huge waste of time. And yet, God says many times in his Word to wait for him. It is an active display of faith as you lay down your desires, hopes, and dreams before the Lord and surrender to his will.

What are you waiting for?

DAY 271

Weak Strength

I will boast all the more gladly about my weaknesses,
so that Christ's power may rest on me.

2 CORINTHIANS 12:9 NIV

You may get impatient with your weakness and insufficiencies, but God doesn't! He doesn't expect you to be strong. He wants you to turn to him in your weakness, so his strength can be yours. Be grateful for your shortcomings and give God a chance to demonstrate his power.

Where can God demonstrate his power in you?

DAY 272

Fixed Gaze

Let your eyes look straight ahead;
fix your gaze directly before you.

PROVERBS 4:25 NIV

Keeping your spiritual eyes focused on what's ahead is even more important than looking up when you're walking. It's easy to search for other resources to meet your needs or solve your problems instead of looking to Jesus. Don't let your gaze wander! Make Jesus your only source.

How do you fix your gaze on Jesus?

DAY 273

Willing to Learn

Teach the older women to live in a way that honors God…
These older women must train the younger women.

Titus 2:3-4 NLT

This admonition is two-fold and potentially problematic. First, the older women must honor God and be willing to teach others. Second, the younger women must be humble and willing to learn. If both groups overcome their hindrances, the blessing of mentorship is incredible!

Who do you teach, and who do you learn from?

REFLECTIONS OF THE WEEK

DAY 274

The Complete Believer

Let endurance have its full effect, so that you may be
mature and complete, lacking nothing.

JAMES 1:4 CSB

You will see your fair share of hard times in this life. In the difficulties, you can develop and grow. God has an eternal perspective, and he is shaping and preparing you for things that are greater than you can imagine. Hold on and trust him.

How have you matured in your spiritual walk?

DAY 275

I Will Help You

I will instruct you and teach you in the way you should go;
I will counsel you with my loving eye on you.

PSALM 32:8 NIV

Sometimes fear becomes so great it starts to control people. What if, instead of being paralyzed by your fears, you told God what you were afraid of? God promises that he will hold your hand, calm your fears, and help you through whatever you're facing.

What do you need God's counsel for today?

DAY 276

Songs of Victory

You protect me from trouble.
You surround me with songs of victory.

Psalm 32:7 NLT

Life can feel like a battle. From keeping up with busy schedules to making major decisions, you are met with daily challenges. Some days you might want to hide away for a while so you can recharge and refocus. God is your hiding place: your protection and your victory. Run to him.

What do you need victory over today?

DAY 277

Questioning Soul

Trust in him at all times, you people;
pour out your hearts to him, for God is your refuge.

Psalm 62:8 NIV

There are questions that you long to have answered by God, and circumstances that leave you wondering about his goodness. What God desires most isn't the soul with the answer; it's the one laid bare before him in trust, belief, and raw vulnerability. He will be your safe place.

What are you questioning today?

DAY 278

Waiting for the Promise

My eyes stay open through the watches of the night,
that I may meditate on your promises.

PSALM 119:148 NIV

What has God promised you? Have you felt his promise through a certain Scripture? Or perhaps through words spoken over your life that cast a vision in your soul? When God promises something, have faith and believe that he will bring it to pass.

What promises are you waiting for?

DAY 279

For You

What, then, shall we say in response to these things?
If God is for us, who can be against us?

ROMANS 8:31 NIV

What a powerful idea that the God of the universe is for you. Don't buy into the untruthful image of God that depicts him as angry, distant, and condemning. His heart toward you has eternally been compassionate, loving, merciful, and tender. Believe it today!

Do you believe that God is for you? Explain.

DAY 280

Comfort

Praise be to the God and Father of your Lord Jesus Christ,
the Father of compassion and the God of all comfort.

2 CORINTHIANS 1:3 NIV

When you face trouble, God doesn't just watch you struggling from a distance. He is your comfort, your strength, and your hope. As he comforts, he also teaches you how to comfort others. You can help someone walk through similar grief as you draw on God's compassion.

Who can you comfort today?

REFLECTIONS OF THE WEEK

DAY 281

Encouraged in Faith

When we get together, I want to encourage you in your faith,
but I also want to be encouraged by yours.

ROMANS 1:12 NLT

True, life-giving friendship will be characterized by a mutual encouragement of faith in Christ. Strive to surround yourself with friends who will point you to Christ and make you long for his presence.

Who are your true friends?

DAY 282

Stronghold

The LORD is good,
A stronghold in the day of trouble.

NAHUM 1:7 NKJV

God isn't only with you when your faith comes easy and your praise is unrestrained. Even in the day of trouble, God knows intimately those who trust him, and he is a stronghold for them. In your moments of hidden weakness, trust him and know that he is always good.

How do you make God your stronghold?

DAY 283

Power of Seeking

You can look for the LORD your God, and you will find him
if you look for him with your whole being.

DEUTERONOMY 4:29 NCV

Do you have days when you feel empty, weary, and uninspired? Days when you feel you have nothing to give, even though there is no shortage of demand. God says that if you look for him with your whole being, you will find him. You can be filled; you just have to seek.

How are you seeking God?

DAY 284

Altar of Sacrifice

By faith Abraham, when he was tested, offered up Isaac.
He received the promises and yet he was offering his one and only son.

HEBREWS 11:17 CSB

Why would God give you vision and a promise and then ask for you to lay that dream down on the altar? It's only in the crucifixion that you find the resurrection. In the laying down and the dying, you find the abundant life of salvation.

How do you trust God with your dreams?

DAY 285

Strength

It is God who arms me with strength
and keeps my way secure.

Psalm 18:32 NIV

God may require you to do something that you don't feel equipped for, but he will always give you what you need to accomplish it. Don't wonder if he chose the wrong person, or if you heard his call correctly! He can enable you to take on any task he asks of you.

What do you think God is asking of you?

DAY 286

Worthy

"You are worthy, O Lord,
To receive glory and honor and power."

Revelation 4:11 NKJV

Worship is a natural response to the goodness of God. It's not simply an emotional reaction; it's also the act of offering back to God the glory he rightly deserves. When you stop to think about God's power, majesty, and creativity, you cannot help but honor him!

How do you worship God?

DAY 287

Return

"The LORD your God is gracious and compassionate, and will not turn His face away from you if you return to Him."

2 CHRONICLES 30:9 NASB

When you have sin in your life, it can be tempting to run from God and hide. You don't want him to see your weakness, and you fear his judgment. Sin creates a barrier between you and God. It blinds you to his mercy and grace. He beckons you to return. He promises compassion.

Do you trust God to be compassionate with you? Explain.

REFLECTIONS OF THE WEEK

DAY 288

What You Say

"Who do you say that I am?" Peter answered and said to Him,
"You are the Christ."

MARK 8:29 NASB

You can follow Jesus, walk with him, even be a devout follower, but who do you truly believe he is? Your belief about who Jesus is has a direct impact on your relationship with him. Jesus' identity won't change no matter what you think. He is the Messiah, the Son of God!

Who do you believe Jesus is?

DAY 289

Eyes Will See

Your eyes will see the King in His beauty;
They will behold a far-distant land.

ISAIAH 33:17 NASB

On days when your faith is weak, your tears flow freely, and your heart is discouraged, you may just wish to see God. The reality of heaven is closer than you can imagine. You will see your King in all his splendor. Every question will be answered and every tear dried.

What do you think God looks like?

DAY 290

Ruled by Emotion

Then we will no longer be immature like children. We won't be tossed and blown about by every wind of new teaching.

Ephesians 4:14 NLT

God has called you to be an overcomer. He desires for you to stand firm in what you know to be true, rather than to be ruled by your varying emotions. As you mature in Christ, the truth of God's Word will come to carry more weight in your heart than your own feelings do.

How much do you allow your emotions to rule?

DAY 291

Unhindered

Because of Christ and your faith in him, you can now come boldly and confidently into God's presence.

Ephesians 3:12 NLT

Your salvation awards you the great privilege of being able to approach God unhindered. With sin no longer dividing you from his holy presence, you are free to bare your soul. There is nothing you cannot share with him. Fear and shame have no place in his excellent love.

Are you unhindered when you approach God?

DAY 292

Focus

I have set the LORD continually before me;
Because He is at my right hand, I will not be shaken.

PSALM 16:8 NASB

The mark of a purposeful life is strong focus. When you fix your eyes on a goal, you are far less likely to become distracted by conflicting interests. By setting the Lord continually before you, you become fixated on the greatest possible purpose.

How do you put God continually before you?

DAY 293

Fulfilling God's Dreams

Only let each person lead the life that the Lord has assigned to him, and to which God has called him. This is my rule in all the churches.

1 CORINTHIANS 7:17 ESV

God created you perfectly to be the person he planned you to be. He has plans for your life and purposes for your talents. By devoting yourself to the life you've been called to, you fulfill God's excellent dream for you. There is no greater privilege than to honor your Creator in this way.

What are God's dreams for you?

DAY 294

Found in a Desert

He found them in a desert, a windy, empty land. He surrounded them and brought them up, guarding them as those he loved very much.

DEUTERONOMY 32:10 NCV

Do you ever go through seasons where you just feel dark? Perhaps directionless or uninspired? In a metaphorical wilderness where you can't get a glimpse of any vision or even hope, God can find you. Even in the desert of your own heart, he can and will meet you.

What season are you in right now?

REFLECTIONS OF THE WEEK

DAY 295

God of Compassion

The LORD is good to everyone.
He showers compassion on all his creation.

PSALM 145:9 NLT

The good things in your life—material, internal, spiritual, or social—are expressions of God's regard for you. When he looks upon you, his heart fills with compassion. He comforts and heals you when you are broken and hurting. If you honestly call on him, he will run to your aide.

How has God's compassion been evident to you?

DAY 296

Death to Life

God… because of His great love with which He loved us, even when we were dead in our transgressions, made us alive together with Christ.

EPHESIANS 2:4 NASB

It's a simple, yet seemingly harsh, law of generation: there must be death for new life to occur. Mirrored by creation, you have things in your life that need to die so you can be alive in Christ. Old habits, negative relationships, damaging thoughts—exchange them now for life!

What things in you need to die?

DAY 297

The End of Death

He will swallow up death forever. The Sovereign LORD
will wipe away the tears from all faces.

ISAIAH 25:8 NIV

How beautiful it is to think that all your fear and shame will someday be erased. Death, the ultimate enemy, will be swallowed up completely when God has his eternal victory. When you put your hope in the Lord, you have the most incredible promise ahead of you!

What most excites you about this promise?

DAY 298

Comfort in Failure

May our Lord Jesus Christ himself and God our Father…
encourage your hearts and strengthen you in every good work and word.

2 THESSALONIANS 2:16-17 CSB

When you feel incapable, God gives you strength to accomplish the task. When you are working sincerely for him, your work—no matter how insignificant it may seem—will always be effective. The work you do for his kingdom is never wasted.

How has God encouraged you to keep going?

DAY 299

Father Knows Best

If we know that he hears us—whatever we ask—
we know that we have what we asked of him.

1 JOHN 5:15 NIV

Your prayers are not offered up to a silent heaven. When you pray, you are heard by a God who cares deeply about what you bring before him. By understanding the depth of his interest, you can gain confidence to approach him boldly in prayer.

How boldly do you approach God?

DAY 300

The Giant Obstacle

"You come against me with a sword, spear, and javelin, but I come against you
in the name of the LORD of Armies, the God of the ranks of Israel."

1 SAMUEL 17:45 CSB

When young David met the champion Goliath in battle, he was so focused on the Lord that the giant who stood before him became nothing more than an obstacle to be overcome. Let God overcome the giants of self-doubt that try to keep you bound in complacency.

What are your giant obstacles?

DAY 301

Kindness to Repentance

"Love your enemies, and do good, and lend, expecting nothing in return... for He Himself is kind to ungrateful and evil men."

LUKE 6:35 NASB

Throughout Scripture the kindness and mercy of God is shown to those who don't deserve it. No one deserves it. God still pursues you with his excellent love regardless of your position. Testify of the grace you've been shown by extending it freely to those in darkness.

How did kindness lead to your repentance?

REFLECTIONS OF THE WEEK

DAY 302

Filling the Emptiness

O God, you are my God; earnestly I seek you;
my soul thirsts for you.

PSALM 63:1 ESV

In times when you aren't sure what you're longing for, it is more of God that you need. Deep in the heart of every person, there is an innate need for intimacy with the Creator. Without it your soul will faint. Ask God to meet you in your emptiness and fill you with his Spirit.

How thirsty are you for God?

DAY 303

Same Spirit

The Spirit of God, who raised Jesus from the dead,
lives in you.

ROMANS 8:11 NLT

The Spirit who reveals mysteries of eternity is the same Spirit who speaks to you. The Spirit who makes dead men live is the same Spirit who brings you to life. As a believer, the Holy Spirit of God literally dwells within you and transforms every facet of your life.

What has the Holy Spirit been speaking to you?

DAY 304

You Make Him Happy

It has pleased the LORD to make you
a people for himself.

1 SAMUEL 12:22 ESV

What could be more rewarding than knowing that you please the Lord? When you enter into a relationship with God, he promises to never leave you. He's with you for the long haul, not only because it's not in his nature to leave, but also because you make him happy.

Is it hard for you to believe this truth? Explain.

DAY 305

Wise Home Construction

"The rain fell, and the floods came, and the winds blew and beat on that house, but it did not fall, because it had been founded on the rock."

MATTHEW 7:24-25 ESV

Every wise builder knows the most important part of building a home is the location of the foundation. The house built on the rock is not immune to violent storms, but it will not be destroyed when they come because it was built on the right foundation.

What foundation have you built your life on?

DAY 306

His Peace

"I leave you peace; my peace I give you. I do not give it to you as the world does. So don't let your hearts be troubled or afraid."

JOHN 14:27 NCV

God waits patiently for his children to draw near so he can impart gifts. He is the only one able to give true peace, and he loves to give it. Receive his gift of peace. It will sustain and satisfy your heart and mind.

When do you experience peace?

DAY 307

Stronger for Waiting

They who wait for the LORD
shall renew their strength.

ISAIAH 40:31 ESV

When you wait, you abdicate your ability to determine when something will happen. When you wait on God, it can be incredibly difficult. Truly waiting on him means you aren't solving situations on your own. If you persevere in waiting, God will renew your strength.

Why do you find it difficult to wait?

DAY 308

Collected Tears

You yourself have recorded my wanderings.
Put my tears in your bottle.

PSALM 56:8 CSB

God isn't absent in your sorrow; he is closer than ever. He collects your tears. Don't be afraid to come to him with your grief. Share the deepest feelings in your heart. In his presence you will find comfort, hope, compassion, and more love than you could imagine.

When do you bring your grief to God?

REFLECTIONS OF THE WEEK

DAY 309

Outwardly Wasting

We do not lose heart. Though outwardly we are wasting away, yet inwardly we are being renewed day by day.

2 CORINTHIANS 4:16 NIV

Aging isn't a valued trait in much of the Western world. Entire industries gross millions of dollars each year to help disguise age. Have you indulged in the lie too? Aging should be honored because it often comes with wisdom which leads to inward renewal and beauty.

What do you think of the aging process?

DAY 310

Light and Momentary

Our light and momentary troubles are achieving for us an eternal glory that far outweighs them all.

2 CORINTHIANS 4:17 NIV

Even though some trouble doesn't seem light at all, the truth is that when it's compared to your eternal glory, it becomes quite small. If you can grasp that this age is temporary and will pass before you know it, then you will weather the troubles that happen here better.

What light and momentary trouble are you in now?

DAY 311

My Gift

Just as each one has received a gift, use it to serve others,
as good stewards of the varied grace of God.

1 PETER 4:10 CSB

Usually gifts are given for the recipient's enjoyment and benefit. In the kingdom of God, a gift is given to a person for the enjoyment and benefit of others. If the Church is to be an example of Christ's love to the world, then selfishness has no place. Serve others with your gifts!

What gifts do you have that can be shared?

DAY 312

Hope of Glory

God has chosen to make known among the Gentiles the glorious riches of this
mystery, which is Christ in you, the hope of glory.

COLOSSIANS 1:27 NIV

If you walk in the knowledge and peace that Christ is in you, by his Spirit, you abide in a place of enormous strength. Jesus is greater than anything and anyone. Acknowledge the powerful truth that if you are born again, Christ is dwelling in you. Indeed, this is the hope of glory.

Where do you place your hope?

DAY 313

Rewards or Wrath

"Store up for yourselves treasures in heaven, where neither moth nor rust destroys, and where thieves do not break in or steal."

MATTHEW 6:20 NASB

In this life you make a direct impact on your life in the age to come. The Bible teaches the principle of storing up various things for the eternal age. Store up treasures and rewards that won't rust, to be enjoyed for all eternity.

What are you storing up?

DAY 314

No Longer Infants

We must become like a mature person, growing until we become like Christ and have his perfection.

EPHESIANS 4:13 NCV

When you first come to Christ, you are a baby in the faith, regardless of your actual age. As God begins his work of making you like him, you mature. Then you can receive and do what he asks without being offended. Don't resist his discipline and training; they are good for you.

How have you matured in your faith?

DAY 315

Mind Control

If people's thinking is controlled by the sinful self, there is death.
But if their thinking is controlled by the Spirit, there is life and peace.

ROMANS 8:6 NCV

No action takes place without starting as a thought. Your mind dictates your entire body. What you give your thoughts to has direct implications on the actions you take. God calls you to be transformed by first renewing your mind so you will rightly discern his will.

How do you control your thoughts?

REFLECTIONS OF THE WEEK

REFLECTIONS

REFLECTIONS

DAY 316

Not Separated

He is the faithful God, keeping his covenant of love to a thousand generations of those who love him and keep his commandments.

DEUTERONOMY 7:9 NIV

Human love is frail. This is why it is all the more critical not to put human attributes on God. His love is nothing like yours. It is steadfast and incapable of failing. Nothing has the power to separate you from it. Be strengthened in his unfailing love today.

How do you measure God's love?

DAY 317

Gift of Weakness

When Uzziah became powerful, his pride led to his ruin. He was unfaithful to the LORD his God.

2 CHRONICLES 26:16 NCV

King Uzziah became King of Judah when he was 16 years old. As long as he sought the Lord, God gave him success. But something changed part way through his reign. His strength became his weakness. It led to pride and his ultimate destruction. Weakness can be a gift.

Can you view your weaknesses as gifts?

DAY 318

Talking Back

Who are you, a human being, to talk back to God? Will what is formed say to the one who formed it, "Why did you make me like this?"

ROMANS 9:20 CSB

God is thick-skinned enough to handle your questions. They don't rattle him or make him insecure. But often they don't help at all. Spiritual maturity is shown when you can whole-heartedly acknowledge that you don't understand God, but you still trust him.

When did you last talk back to God?

DAY 319

The Bigger Picture

"Where were you when I established the earth? Tell me, if you have understanding."

JOB 38:4 CSB

Often God uses, and sometimes even creates storms so he can have your undivided attention. If God was capable of orchestrating the intricate design of the earth, then surely he is capable of leading your life with the same care and wisdom. Listen for his voice in your storm.

How can you look at the bigger picture?

DAY 320

Discipline as a Gift

No discipline seems pleasant at the time, but painful. Later on, however, it produces a harvest of righteousness and peace.

HEBREWS 12:11 NIV

Children who have learned healthy submission are a delight to be around. They exhibit obedience to rules and authority even when they don't like it. If you submit to the discipline of God in your life, you will reap a harvest of righteousness and peace.

How can you submit to God's discipline?

DAY 321

Running Unhindered

Since we are surrounded by such a great cloud of witnesses, let us throw off everything that hinders and the sin that so easily entangles.

HEBREWS 12:1 NIV

In the Olympics, do you see runners racing with a backpack on their back? Hiking boots, jeans, coats, or sweatshirts? No. Their goal is to not be hindered by anything so they can run the best possible race. You have the power to make your run much easier: listen to the Holy Spirit.

What might be hindering you?

DAY 322

God Loves Justice

Let the fear of the Lord be upon you. Judge carefully, for with the Lord your God there is no injustice or partiality or bribery.

2 Chronicles 19:7 NIV

Do you long for justice? You must know that your passion for justice comes from God's heart. Not everything looks fair and equitable right now. But this isn't the end. Your just Judge will judge the world rightly when all is said and done.

What does justice look like to you?

REFLECTIONS OF THE WEEK

DAY 323

Stored Goodness

How abundant are the good things
that you have stored up for those who fear you.

PSALM 31:19 NIV

What are the abundant good things God has in store? Safety and security? Peace in trials? A quiet heart in the middle of a storm? Joy in mourning? It would seem that his goodness could be all of these and much more. When you fear the Lord, it can all be yours.

What good things are you hoping for?

DAY 324

Learn from Me

"Come to me, all you who are weary and burdened,
and I will give you rest."

MATTHEW 11:28 NIV

Perhaps it's morning. Your day is just beginning, yet your heart is already heavy. Or maybe it's the end of the day, and you feel weakened by the burdens you have taken on. Rest in the kindest person there ever was. Let his words soothe and strengthen you.

What burdens can you give to God today?

DAY 325

A Friend in Him

"I have called you friends, for everything that I learned from my Father I have made known to you."

JOHN 15:15 NIV

Have you ever found yourself obeying the commands of God with a heart that was far from his? Of being a rule-keeper without walking in deep friendship with him? God is looking for a friendship with you. He wants to share deep and wonderful things with you.

How can you be a better friend to God?

DAY 326

Ask Seek Knock

"Ask and it will be given to you; seek and you will find; knock and the door will be opened to you."

MATTHEW 7:7 NIV

God promises to work everything out for good in your heart and life. Don't let your disappointments cloud the truth. Everyone who asks in his name receives. He promises you will find him. He will open the door to you. Trust the promises in his Word.

What are you asking God for?

DAY 327

Calling and Selection

Be all the more diligent to make certain
about His calling and choosing you.

2 PETER 1:10 NASB

Requiring a journey from faith to love is impossible, but to live and dwell in Christ makes for a fully satisfying, joy-filled journey. When you stumble, Jesus helps you up. When you are weak, he is strong. Assess your heart, and trust Jesus to it.

Are you certain of God's calling?

DAY 328

Growing in Discernment

See to it that no one takes you captive
through philosophy and empty deception.

COLOSSIANS 2:8 NASB

The simplicity of the gospel can be offensive. This is because it relies solely on Jesus' complete work on the cross and not on merit. There are many false teachings that will try to lead you away from simple faith. Stay rooted and grounded in the teachings of Jesus so you don't fall.

How can you grow in discernment?

DAY 329

The Process

Put on your new nature, and be renewed as you learn to know your Creator and become like him.

COLOSSIANS 3:10 NLT

While your salvation is a completed work, there is a continual working out of your faith. This is because God has called you into a relationship. After salvation, you are renewed through continuing to repent and submit yourself to God. Keep going! He is committed to the process.

What does your renewal process look like?

REFLECTIONS OF THE WEEK

DAY 330

Content Always

I have learned how to be content
with whatever I have.

PHILIPPIANS 4:11 NLT

The secret to contentment is realizing that your circumstances don't determine your peace. You might be suffering, or you might be on a mountaintop of victory, but your peace and your steadfast walk with God remain the same. Be satisfied that God will give you what you need.

How content are you?

DAY 331

Standing Blameless

To Him who is able to keep you from stumbling, and to make you
stand in the presence of His glory blameless with great joy.

JUDE 1:24 NASB

How do you suppose you will react upon seeing God? He calls you to stand before him. How will you even breathe? That you can stand blameless with great joy is an amazing truth that should cause you to shed tears of gratitude. He considers you blameless because of Jesus.

How do you feel about standing before God?

DAY 332

A Confident Approach

Let us then approach God's throne of grace with confidence, so that we may receive mercy and find grace to help us in our time of need.

HEBREWS 4:16 NIV

If there is an urgent need or difficult situation, nothing delights a parent more than their child running to them for help. That is a small picture of what God wants you to do with him. God invites you to confidently approach his throne. Don't be afraid.

How will you approach God today?

DAY 333

Origin of Strength

"People do not live by bread alone, but by every word that comes from the mouth of God."

MATTHEW 4:4 NLT

It's interesting how God prepared Jesus for this trial. He didn't have him attend a conference, read a self-help book, or have a healing service. Instead, he led his Son to be physically weaker so he could lean fully on the Father.

Have you seen the benefits of fasting?

DAY 334

The First Move

We love because
he first loved us.

1 JOHN 4:19 NIV

God loves you just because you are his. And you love him because he loved you. It's just that simple. He made the first move, and now you can follow his lead. Be restored and refreshed by his pure and perfect love.

How do you show God love?

DAY 335

The Eternal Gift

"Give glory to God in heaven, and on earth let there be peace
among the people who please God."

LUKE 2:14 NCV

Christ's mission is to redeem you from every thought, word, and action that doesn't match up to your Godlikeness. He destroyed your sins and silenced your enemy, permanently, on the cross. He empowered you for victory. This is his eternal gift to you.

How can you glorify God?

DAY 336

Execute Your Hope

"Do not come near it, that you may know the way by which you shall go, for you have not passed this way before."

JOSHUA 3:4 NASB

The Lord had spoken; the Israelites would consecrate themselves and follow the Ark of the Covenant into their promise. You face daily decisions that position you toward the fulfillment of God's promises in your life. Take courage, consecrate yourself, and follow him.

How will you execute your hope today?

REFLECTIONS OF THE WEEK

DAY 337

The Love-Joy Life

"These things I have spoken to you, that my joy may be in you,
and that your joy may be full."

JOHN 15:11 ESV

Joy comes into your life through actions of obedience. You may obey God for the sake of righteousness, but God rewards you for it by baptizing you in his love! As you abide in this love, you become a vessel of joy, spilling onto dry places in the world around you.

How full is your joy today?

DAY 338

Water of Life

"The water that I shall give him will become in him
a fountain of water springing up into everlasting life."

JOHN 4:14 NKJV

Sometimes, you need extra. Spiritual requirements are never met by earthly experiences. Jesus says he brings abundant life wherever the enemy has tried to kill, steal, or destroy. He is just that faithful. His living water is an endless fountain. Rely on him to fill you with this eternal life.

Are you drinking living water?

DAY 339

False Expectations

This is how you know what love is: Jesus Christ laid down his life for us. And you ought to lay down your lives for your brothers and sisters.

1 John 3:16 NIV

Part of laying down your life rests in relinquishing misplaced expectations. When the highlight reel of your mind doesn't match your life, you hand that reel to Jesus. He returns belonging and peace. You are not a failure. You are a possibility.

What expectations do you have for life?

DAY 340

Charity

Dear children, let us not love with words or speech but with actions and in truth.

1 John 3:18 NIV

In a time of hope and gladness, your active love reaches beyond the circumstances of the afflicted. Use your hands and your supply to bless the hearts of those who are in need. You can show the love of Jesus through giving of yourself.

Who can you be charitable toward?

DAY 341

Freed for Life

"Let any one of you who is without sin
be the first to throw a stone at her."

JOHN 8:7 NIV

If you feel Jesus is holding back his love and compassion from you because of something you have done or not done, think again! God isn't hung up on your sin; he hung your sin on a cross and set you free! Enjoy living.

How do you enjoy your freedom from sin?

DAY 342

Known

"You know neither Me nor My Father; if you knew Me,
you would know My Father also."

JOHN 8:19 NASB

You are a stranger to this world, and because you inhabit it, all heaven breaks loose, and the earth gets set on its head. You might not see this for yourself, but it's true. That annoys some people as much as it blesses the rest. Take courage! Jesus sees and understands you.

How do you remain a stranger to the things of the world?

DAY 343

Steps to Intimacy

It is he who made us, and you are his;
you are his people, the sheep of his pasture.

PSALM 100:3 NIV

King David celebrated God. He worshiped him gladly, singing songs to him. This sets David's heart in proper perspective. When you encounter God's worthiness, you should experience gratitude, and echo that back to God.

What praise can you offer God today?

REFLECTIONS OF THE WEEK

DAY 344

God Provides

"Behold, I have given you every plant yielding seed…
and every tree which has fruit yielding seed; it shall be food for you."

GENESIS 1:29 NASB

God gave the first recursive gift: plants which bear seeds. He then said to multiply and farm the land. You plant, you water, you weed, yet God creates the miracle. You can take delight in playing a very small part in your providence. God loves to collaborate with you.

What food are you especially grateful for?

DAY 345

Emotions

There is an appointed time for everything.
And there is a time for every event under heaven.

ECCLESIASTES 3:1 NASB

God's emotions are on full display throughout Scripture. He made you in his image. He understands your form and your emotions. He teaches you when to express or conceal them, and to administer your responses in righteousness. He leads you into emotional freedom.

How do you handle your emotions?

DAY 346

Making Choices

The Lord God caused to grow… the tree of life also in the midst of the garden, and the tree of the knowledge of good and evil.

Genesis 2:9 NASB

God created the tree of life. He made all things good. How was the tree of the knowledge of good and evil good? Because it gave you a choice. Just like you can't make anyone love you, God won't try to make you love or obey him. These are choices you make for yourself.

How do you choose God?

DAY 347

Acceptance

"I have brought you glory on earth by finishing the work you gave me to do."

John 17:4 NIV

As you walk in love, you will see fruit develop from what you do. Sometimes your gifts are a portion of a legacy that cannot be recognized in a generation. The point is this: you are being faithful. God is proud of you for bringing him glory.

How can you bring glory to God today?

DAY 348

Triune God

In the beginning was the Word, and the Word was with God,
and the Word was God. He was with God in the beginning.

John 1:1-2 CSB

The triune God is a little like a chocolate bar. Each piece is part of the whole, but whole as a part. Whether he breaks off a piece that comes to earth, or enters the person who believes, if you have experienced him in one form, you have experienced him in all three.

How do you understand the Trinity?

DAY 349

Eternally Blessed

How blessed is the man who fears the Lord,
Who greatly delights in His commandments.

Psalm 112:1 NASB

Blessings from God are gifts given as a result of his grace. You can grow in God's graces just as you grow in the graces of the people around you. When you revere him and abide in his love, your heart knits together with his, and you experience his delight.

What does it look like to delight in God's commands?

DAY 350

Filling the Hole

"Where your treasure is,
there your heart will be also."

MATTHEW 6:21 CSB

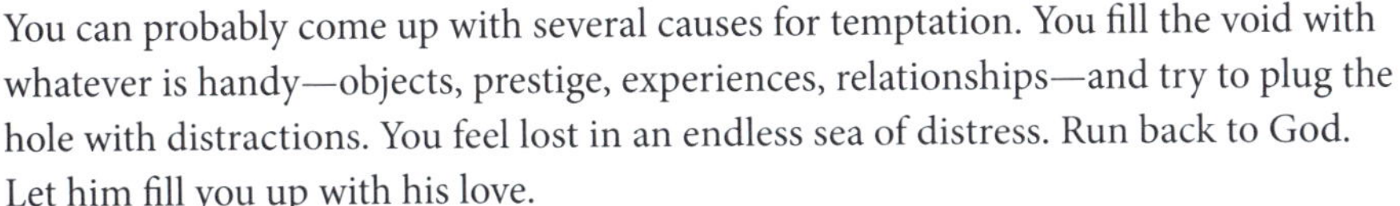

You can probably come up with several causes for temptation. You fill the void with whatever is handy—objects, prestige, experiences, relationships—and try to plug the hole with distractions. You feel lost in an endless sea of distress. Run back to God. Let him fill you up with his love.

Where is your treasure?

REFLECTIONS OF THE WEEK

DAY 351

The Proper Time

"There is only one thing worth being concerned about.
Mary has discovered it, and it will not be taken away from her."

LUKE 10:41-42 NLT

Martha's problem was not that she was a hard worker but that she neglected the correct choice. If God wants to speak with you personally, it is time to drop everything and listen. Sit at his feet, and let him provide for you.

What are you most concerned about?

DAY 352

He Delights in You

The LORD directs the steps of the godly.
He delights in every detail of their lives.

PSALM 37:23 NLT

Jesus lives in you by choice. He has saved you quite capably. He is excited merely by being with you. He promises to calm your fears and direct your steps. He is so happy that you exist that the very joy of it causes him to burst forth into singing as he delights in the details of your life.

How do you delight in God?

DAY 353

Blessed Enemies

If your enemy is hungry, feed him. If he is thirsty, give him something to drink.
For in so doing you will be heaping fiery coals on his head.

ROMANS 12:20 CSB

When you heap kindness on people who hurt you, they notice the disparity between their actions and your mercy. As the flames of mercy spring up for a cold heart, you create opportunities for reconciliation and peace.

How can you offer kindness today?

DAY 354

Illuminated Motives

A plan in the heart of a man is like deep water,
But a man of understanding draws it out.

PROVERBS 20:5 NASB

It's difficult to understand people's motives. They get in your face, grate on your nerves, and disrupt your peace. The Bible says you need understanding to figure people out. Be pure-hearted and receptive as you pursue, and you will learn a great deal.

How can you try to understand someone better?

DAY 355

Undeserved Kindness

David asked, "Is there anyone still left of the house of Saul to whom I can show kindness for Jonathan's sake?"

2 SAMUEL 9:1 NIV

Because of Saul's cruelty to David, Mephibosheth would have been an unlikely candidate for David's kindness. But David extended luxurious favor upon Jonathan's son without benefit to himself. You may feel you have little to offer, but Jesus invites you to his table every day.

Who can you show undeserved kindness to?

DAY 356

Dressed for Weather

Put on the new self, created to be like God in true righteousness and holiness.

EPHESIANS 4:24 NIV

What a blessing it is that you will affect people by just being you: lovely, holy, and loved of God. Earth isn't your home; life here is laden with storms. Fortunately, God has given you clothes for the weather. Put them on and stand in his protective warmth.

How can you dress for the weather?

DAY 357

As You Are

God chose what is foolish in the world to shame the wise;
God chose what is weak in the world to shame the strong.

1 Corinthians 1:27-28 esv

God is so pleased with you walking in his trust that he uses you to make his name great in unlikely places. You wouldn't be able to go in your own strength, and a lot of things wouldn't necessarily make sense. Ask him to lead you in his way, and you will succeed.

What things of God seem foolish at first?

REFLECTIONS OF THE WEEK

DAY 358

Boldly Proclaim

When they had seen him, they spread the word concerning what had been told them about this child, and all who heard it were amazed.

LUKE 2:16-18 NIV

When the shepherds were told about Jesus, they didn't pencil him into their schedules; they ran as fast as their feet could carry them. Once they saw him, they rushed to tell others about him. Christ has come! Tell your friends! Tell your neighbors! Tell everyone you meet.

Who can you tell about Jesus today?

DAY 359

No Expiration

May the God of hope fill you with all joy and peace as you trust in him, so that you may overflow with hope by the power of the Holy Spirit.

ROMANS 15:13 NIV

Jesus, a Jew, came so all people would be qualified to experience his indescribable hope, joy, and peace as they placed their faith in him. It's no wonder a great band of angels joined together in praise that night. Jesus is the true basis for every believer's hope and joy.

Do you find your joy and peace in Jesus?

DAY 360

No Returns

God never changes his mind about the people he calls
and the things he gives them.

ROMANS 11:29 NCV

Isn't it refreshing that God, in his great understanding and thoughtfulness, gives gifts appropriate and specific to you: gifts that do not cause regret? Moreover, these often produce more gifts that you can give to the world, and back to God.

How can you begin the journey God is calling you to?

DAY 361

Free from Anger

People with understanding control their anger;
a hot temper shows great foolishness.

PROVERBS 14:29 NLT

Anger is a response to suppressed fear, humiliation, rejection, or pain. Getting to the root of these events allows you to deal with anger, disarm, and move forward, unencumbered. Jesus isn't cruel: he doesn't want you to be mishandled. He will reward you as you submit to him.

How do you control your anger?

DAY 362

Steadfast Hope

We know that in all things God works for the good of those who love him, who have been called according to his purpose.

ROMANS 8:28 NIV

Not everything starts out being God's idea for your life, but he makes beauty in spite of that. The good God has in mind might not even be on your radar. But if the love of God is peaceable and kind, then surely his gifts are in step with that.

What good is God working in your life?

DAY 363

Source of Beauty

Don't let your beauty consist of outward things… but rather what is inside the heart—the imperishable quality of a gentle and quiet spirit.

1 PETER 3:3-4 CSB

Beauty shines from within. It dresses in humility and wisdom. It grows in an environment of reverent, holy living, thriving in worship and glorifying God. It is good to look nice, and sometimes your gifts or calling require it, but keep holiness your central focus for true beauty.

Where is your source of beauty?

DAY 364

Law of the Spirit

"I will put My laws into their hearts,
and in their minds I will write them."

HEBREWS 10:16 NKJV

The year Christ was crucified at Passover, his disciples were gathered in the Upper Room. The promised Holy Spirit came and filled them, thus writing the law of the Spirit in their hearts. The Holy Spirit lives in those who believe, speaking the Word of God into their hearts.

What is written on your heart?

DAY 365

Load of Anxiety

Don't worry about anything, but in everything, through prayer and petition
with thanksgiving, present your requests to God.

PHILIPPIANS 4:6 CSB

Carrying anxiety is like over-packing a car for a trip. Gas mileage suffers, companions have a hard time joining you, and blocked vision creates added danger. What is the key to shaking anxiety? Rejoice in God and gratefully request his help. There's no room for anxiety with him!

What anxieties do you need to unpack?

REFLECTIONS